the
Responsible
Society

the
Responsible
Society

Stephen Roman
and
Eugen Loebl

Regina Ryan Books/
Two Continents Publishing Group, Ltd.
New York   1977

Printed in the U.S.A.
Regina Ryan Books/
Two Continents
30 East 42nd Street
New York, New York 10017

Library of Congress Cataloging in Publication Data
Roman, Stephen
    The responsible society.
    1. Economic policy.   2. Social policy.
I. Loebl, Eugen, 1907–   joint author.
II. Title.
HD82.R67   338.9   77–9155
ISBN 0–8467–0360–2
LCCN 77–9155

A Note
From
The Publisher

When I first heard about the collaboration between Eugen Loebl and Stephen Roman, I was astonished at the idea that men of such contrasting backgrounds would be able to agree on an economic philosophy. What, possibly, I asked myself, could a former high-ranking Communist government official and a multimillionaire businessman, who is a key figure in the "capitalist establishment," find in common one with the other? How could they have arrived, separately, at the same conclusions about what is wrong with our economy? And how could they have worked together so closely to formulate a solution to these problems, coming as they did from opposite poles of thought and life?

Yet, Mr. Roman, chairman of the board and chief executive officer of a business based on one of the world's largest uranium mines, and Professor Loebl, former head of the Ministry of Foreign Trade in Czechoslovakia and a former leading Marxist theoretician, had written a book that seemed to me to have great significance for the future well-being of our planet. As I worked with them, preparing the book for publication, the story behind their unusual collaboration gradually unfolded for me. And I began to feel strongly that this story provides an important dimension to an appreciation and understanding of *The Responsible Society*—and should be shared with the reader.

Both were born in Slovakia—Loebl in 1907, Roman in 1921. The son of a Catholic farmer, Roman emigrated to Canada in 1937 at the age of sixteen. He worked first on a farm in central Ontario, then on an assembly line along the northern shores of Lake Ontario. Meanwhile, Loebl, the son of a Jewish merchant and a graduate of the University of World Trade, in Vienna, was moving up in the ranks of the Czecho-Slovak Communist Party; by the 1930s he was one of the nation's most important Marxist economists.

During World War II, while Roman served in the Canadian Army, Loebl was in London, as head of the Ministry of Economic Reconstruction of the Czecho-Slovak Government in Exile. After the war, Roman became editor of a Slovak-language newspaper in the Toronto area; and he began to build the foundation of his business, organizing a mining group, which successfully developed oil and gas interests in Western Canada and the Williston Basin of North Dakota. Meanwhile, Loebl became a member of the Council of Economic Advisers of the Politburo and chief of the Czecho-Slovak Ministry of Foreign Trade. Each man was rising, seemingly inexorably, to the top of his respective ladder—one in the free-enterprise system, the other in the Communist system.

But while Roman's business interests continued to grow —to the point where he acquired and developed the property now known as Denison Mines, Ltd., at Elliot Lake, in northern Ontario, into the largest uranium mine in the world—Loebl was running head-on into conflict with the Soviet Union over his plan to help rebuild his country by trading with the United States and the nations of Western Europe. He was arrested in 1949, thrown into jail, interrogated brutally by Soviet intelligence officers, and forced to confess to a variety of fictionalized "crimes"—namely, of being pro-Western, an "internationalist," and a "cosmopolitan." Then he was paraded out for the infamous anti-Semitic Slansky Trials of 1952 and sentenced to life imprisonment. During his five years of solitary confinement, he set about systematically to rethink the theories of communism and capitalism—and to develop an alternative system of economics, which he calls Humanomics. (The story of his imprisonment is told in *My Mind on Trial,* A Helen and Kurt Wolff Book, 1976. The basic theory of Humanomics is set forth in the Random House book *Humanomics,* also published in 1976.)

After eleven years in prison, Loebl was released on probation. After three years of forced labor, he was rehabilitated through the intercession of Alexander Dubcek and appointed Director of the State Bank. When the Soviets invaded Czechoslovakia in 1968, he decided he had to get out. He escaped to Germany, then emigrated to the United States. In 1969, he served for one semester as professor of economics at the University of Southern Illinois, in Carbondale; then was appointed professor of economics and political science at Vassar College, where he taught until his retirement in June of 1976.

The two men first met in the spring of 1974 in New York City through Slovak friends. They discussed social and economic problems and, surprisingly, both the critique and the remedy they envisaged were practically identical.

The difference was only in their point of departure. While Roman saw the problems through the prism of the Judeo-Christian philosophy of man, his practical experience and his remarkable common sense, Loebl came to his conclusion as a critique of the theories of Adam Smith and Karl Marx, and their followers today.

Loebl, though respectful of his Jewish heritage and its teachings, had originally not thought in these terms. He was at first perplexed and then profoundly stirred by Roman's approach. Loebl saw that his theories were actually deeply rooted in the Judeo-Christian value system and that it might present a way to place these ethical teachings—particularly the command to love one's neighbor, and the corresponding imperative to take responsibility for one's fellow human beings—at the philosophical center of a new economic theory. And, since ideas have consequences, the plans and mechanisms developed from such an economic philosophy would reinforce these ethical values right down to the day-to-day workings of the economy.

Together, over the next three years, one of the most successful industrialists in the world—the man of common sense —and one of the most respected economists of our time—the visionary philosopher—worked on this unusual project. The result is a program of simple, practical steps that, if implemented, could lead to an economy without inflation, unemployment, ecological catastrophe, and unjust distribution of income—"where human beings are at the center of all considerations."

This, then, is *The Responsible Society*.

New York   REGINA RYAN
June, 1977

Contents

Credo

The decades of the sixties and the seventies have brought with them a time of crisis for the nations of the Western world. While the outstanding features of this crisis are economic and social, its roots penetrate to the heart of Western culture. It is my belief that we are facing not only social and economic tragedy but also, and more important, a tragedy for all of Western civilization. The ideals and values from which this civilization emerged have become lost in a flurry of scientific and technological development, and the products of this development, while designed to serve man, have become a threat to his existence.

A crisis of this magnitude cannot be understood by focusing only on the socioeconomic problems that characterize it. Inflation, unemployment, crime, depersonalization— these are symptoms of the disease but not its causes. In order to understand the true nature of this crisis and the reasons for the tragic decline we are in, I believe we must turn to the doctrines and beliefs that have formed the base from which Western civilization and its great achievements emerged.

Of all the cultures and traditions that have influenced the development of Western civilization, it is my feeling that none has had a more profound effect upon us than that of the Judeo-Christian philosophy of man. In this system of beliefs, man is regarded as the greatest of creatures, made in the image and likeness of God. God created nature *for* man; man was made a part of nature but endowed with the genius of creativity; he was also given the responsibility to transform his manmade and God-given environment into God's Kingdom on Earth.

> So God created man in his own image . . . male and
> female he created them.
> And God blessed them and said to them, "Be fruitful
> and multiply, and fill the earth and subdue it; and
> have dominion over the fish of the sea and over

the birds of the air and over every living thing
that moves upon the earth."

And God said, "Behold, I have given you every plant
yielding seed which is upon the face of all the earth,
and every tree with seed in its fruit; you shall have
them for food."

(Genesis: 1.27–29)

Since the earth has been given to us to be subdued, we
have to see work as the responsibility of all of us: "If any man
will not work neither let him eat" was the judgment of Saint
Paul (Second Letter to the Thessalonians: 3.2). Likewise, the
fruits of our labor should benefit all.

Looking back over the history of Western civilization,
we can interpret the development of humanity and society as a
gradual mastering of nature and the forces inherent in her.
From this perspective, man has moved from the primitive
stage of absolute dependency on nature to the present one of
the control and utilization of natural forces for his own benefit. He has succeeded to a great extent in realizing the role
assigned to him by God according to Judeo-Christian philosophy. Yet in doing so man has to face a socioeconomic
paradox, that he cannot achieve greater freedom from the
forces of nature without its limitation by corresponding responsibility.

From another angle, the history of Western civilization
is also a history of violations of one of the highest ideals
and values of this philosophy. In the Judeo-Christian tradition, the imperative "Love thy neighbor as thyself" should
govern all actions of man, even the mastering of nature. As
one of the greatest of God's commandments (Matthew: 22.
39), the ability to love one's fellow man, to feel responsibility
for others, takes on the highest ethical and moral value and
serves as a measure of man's greatness. Yet throughout the
history of Western civilization, man's freedom, his dignity,

his responsibility for his environment—all the noble qualities and roles attributed to him in this philosophy have been ruthlessly undermined by individuals or institutions, despite their professed belief in it.

This contradiction in the development of Western man is most obvious in our own century. The past seventy years have brought forth some of the greatest triumphs of Western civilization and, at the same time, some of the most horrifying manmade tragedies. The totalitarian regimes of Hitler and Stalin, with their unprecedented instances of class and racial hatred, the two world wars, are all examples of the flagrant disregard of the Judeo-Christian concept of the brotherhood of man.

Certainly, this trend away from the Judeo-Christian ethic in regard to man's treatment of man continues in the present. Even our perception of the obvious signs of the crisis confronting our society is permeated with this anti-human attitude. Our society and its economy are viewed as a system of commodities rather than of human beings. Gross national product, rate of interest, of profit, of unemployment and inflation have become the center of our economic considerations rather than the people who make such figures possible. Even the traditional means of showing one's concern for those less fortunate than oneself, charity, has come to be regarded as a tax deduction rather than an act of giving, and we have turned the responsibility for the poor and helpless over to a heartless bureaucratic apparatus. Finally, this bureaucracy, the national government, conceived as an organ of the people, has alienated itself from those it should serve and further dehumanizes our society.

This, then, is what I believe to be the essence and root of the socioeconomic crisis endangering the foundations of Western civilization: Primarily bound to Judeo-Christian culture, we have developed societies based on a contradiction; for while we have followed God's injunction to master nature, and have greatly increased our ability to control nature and her forces, we have disregarded God's commandment to love and feel responsibility for our fellow man. Although the ideals of the Judeo-Christian philosophy have been all but eliminated from the day-to-day working of our social system, it is also my belief that, as human beings living in a culture whose roots spring from this philosophy, deep in our hearts we long to see these most human ideals resurrected. In fact, even those social thinkers, and particularly economists, who advocate theories and practices supporting a mechanized society devoid of all human values attempt to adhere to these values in their daily lives.

It is from these thoughts and feelings, out of the hopes and fears of both Mr. Loebl and myself, that *The Responsible Society* has emerged. In it, we have attempted to reinterpret the complexity of our economy and the society that supports it in terms of the Judeo-Christian concept of humanity. Through this work, we hope that the road will be found to an economy in which human beings, with their material and spiritual needs, will become the center of all considerations —a road to a socioeconomic system oriented toward, rather than against, humankind. With this in mind, our book addresses itself to the countless millions of people who long for human dignity and responsibility.

Thus, the task of *The Responsible Society* is to project the principles and values of the Judeo-Christian philosophy both in theory and practice into our economy. It always was and always will be of crucial importance that each of us should be guided by the great ethical imperatives of this philosophy; but we must be aware that for a modern society the behavior of the individual can be, and is to a great degree, influenced by his social and economic system.

In a responsible society, we understand a society of human beings responsible to God, to God's commandments, to each other and to society—but also the responsibility of the society and its government toward the people. We do not think a society is responsible if it degrades people willing to work, willing to create what is needed, to the state of unemployment. Nor is it responsible when earnings for good work are paid in bad money that, through inflation, loses its purchasing power. The power of the government has to be derived not from the simple act of elections but from its responsibility and its duty toward the nation.

To create full employment, a stable currency, a healthy environment, sharing of profit, harmony between capital and labor—that is our concept of the responsible society.

It is the task of this book to show that such an avenue is not only necessary but possible.

It is, to our knowledge, the first attempt to project the Judeo-Christian philosophy into the orientation and behavior of the socioeconomic system as such. Consequently, it should be regarded as a challenge, not a final blueprint.

For my part, I am fully aware that the task of working out *comprehensive* programs for the establishment and achievement of goals in a given economic system is still ahead of us. Our concern was to work out a kind of charter that would offer solutions to the most burning problems that could be implemented *immediately*. Thus, even if only a few steps could be taken, these steps will be headed in the right direction. Let us act now—before it is too late.

Toronto   STEPHEN ROMAN
April, 1977

Introduction

We are accustomed to seeing the world divided into two economic systems: that of Adam Smith and that of Karl Marx. We assume not just that they are real alternatives but also that they are the only alternatives. Let us examine the bases of these two systems to see whether in fact either of these assumptions is correct.

The theoretical founder of capitalism, the moral philosopher Adam Smith, advocated a society and economy of free human beings and free enterprise. He believed that self-interest and the propensity to barter were the basic motivations for economic activities. Still he concluded that, despite these selfish motivations, their effect would be harmonized "as if by an invisible hand" to benefit all.

Why did this philosophy of humanism when applied to what we call "capitalism" turn against humanity and create the grave social and economic crisis we are facing? Where did capitalism go astray? How is it that this philosophy proposed by a deeply religious moral philosopher did not meet its goals?

Smith's point of departure was that if all enterprises concerned themselves with just their own interest, an "invisible hand" would harmonize the economic performance of the nation. But the depression of the 1930s showed that the "invisible hand" is unable to perform this function. Smith's theoretical assumptions must have been wrong.

More than a century after Smith, John Maynard Keynes continued to accept the role of the "invisible hand," with his concept of the self-recuperating ability of a free enterprise system. However, Keynes felt that the free enterprise system needed the assistance of a "visible hand," that of the government. He claimed that simply through government spending unemployment would be eliminated, a goal which the "invisible hand" alone could not achieve. As Keynes' ideas have become the dominant philosophy of capitalism, the "visible hand" of the government has become more and more powerful, and its interference has had a deadening impact on the free enterprise system. Freedom of enterprise has permanently diminished, unemployment has not been eradicated, and inflation has been added to the original malaise.

Once we look at the economy from the point of view of the Judeo-Christian philosophy, it will become clear where Smith, Keynes and capitalism went astray.

In the Judeo-Christian philosophy humans cannot be reduced to selfishness and the propensity to barter. Undoubtedly, all too many people may have these properties, and the properties may play an important role in our lives and in the economy. Still, human beings have other properties as well—spiritual needs, a sense of beauty, justice, the ability to think and create, to have emotions, to be able to love and hate, to dream and to be rational, to have passions and a will. All these properties of human beings determine their actions and their reactions to their social and natural environment, and the economy cannot be understood without perceiving real human beings. The economy must therefore be seen as a system of total human beings with all their spiritual and material needs and their ability to think. From this it follows that the economy—as a human system—must be harmonized by those who created it: it is we human beings who are the creators of the economic system, and we have the responsibility to harmonize its performance. This principle applies also to the concept of free enterprise by which we mean free business, free workers, free consumers. We have to create conditions under which all these areas of free enterprise will flourish. If we find that we need the assistance of the government it should only be involved with the creation of such conditions—without interfering with the performance of the enterprise.

The system based on the philosophy of Marx accepts the same ideas, even though it reaches different conclusions. Marx also accepted the existence of laws more or less identical with those of nature, and perceived the history of humankind as the history of class struggle. He disregarded our dreams of freedom and happiness and relegated human beings to classes. The properties of classes and not those of human beings play the essential role in Marx's economy. The form of ownership is supposed to determine human behavior; presumably, then, a more humane society will emerge if we change the form of ownership of the means of production.

According to Marx, the main task is not fighting for humanism and developing a more humane society, nor making the means of production and nature serve us, but the other way around. We will become humane as a kind of by-product in changing the form of ownership.

Marx accepted the idea that the history of humankind is determined by eternal laws. Consequently, he felt that socialism must replace capitalism with the inevitability of natural law. The very concept of human responsibility for the development of society is neglected. The agent of this historical change is the class of manual workers. Not developing science, art, philosophy, human creativity, but brute manual labor is supposed to be the determining historical force. Marx's notion that it is the mission of history to replace capitalism with socialism-communism is the ideological justification for destroying everybody who objects to this "absolute and eternal law." It justifies the dictatorship of the "historical agent," the proletariat. The catastrophe that Marx's philosophy brought on humankind is no deviation from his idea but the very consequence of its application.

Both systems contradict the very essence of the Judeo-Christian philosophy. This applies not only to the deeply religious moral philosopher Adam Smith but also to the atheist scholar Marx, who deeply sympathized with the dehumanized victims of the system he observed.

In projecting the Judeo-Christian philosophy into economics and social science generally, we differ from the above philosophies and the economic theories derived from them. We see society and the economy as a creation of thinking human beings and therefore as the responsibility of human beings. We will not rely on so-called economic laws, we will not accept the idea that the malaise of our society is inevitable. We will not look at the economy as a boat without a navigator and leave it to the waves to determine where and how and when it lands.

Thus, in our study, we will not merely present a critique of traditional economics, but we will put forth positive measures that, if followed, would lead to the humanization of our economy. These measures would guarantee full employment, the stable purchasing power of our currency, and a concern for the natural environment and the scarce resources needed for future generations.

Our tools for achieving these goals will be totally new concepts of money, credit, and taxation. We will replace government spending with government lending. And we will introduce a new concept of profit-sharing. These measures are not mere technical devices; they grow out of and are an integral part of our new approach to economics.

Thus, we will have to question many accepted concepts. We will have to formulate new tasks for the government, and we will prove that the existing economic theories abandoned the basics of the Judeo-Christian philosophy of man, to the peril of our civilization. And we will show that when we project the values of this philosophy into economic theories and concepts, we may create a humane society dominating nature for the benefit of all human beings in this world.

the
Responsible
Society

1
Economics and Common Sense

$600 Million Lost Per Day

The Western world possesses an advanced and sophisticated technology. This technology has raised the standard of living and the level of education and culture for the entire world to an unprecedented degree, and is capable of creating a real utopia for humankind. Yet suddenly our technological and cultural advance is coming to a standstill. Our potential for greatness remains, but what has been termed "the current economic crisis" leaves us with little hope of achieving that potential.

The situation that confronts us borders on the absurd. There are laborers, scientists, and professional people with the ability to create wealth for their own developed nations and to help those that are still underdeveloped, but they are not given the opportunity to do so. People need housing, yet construction workers are unemployed; people need education, yet teachers cannot find work; people need thousands of goods, yet those who could produce them fill the welfare lines.

The statistics reveal how incredible the situation is. The total production of goods and services in 1977 has fallen far below the level of 1973. The take-home pay of the average blue-collar worker is 6 to 7 percent lower in purchasing power than it was a year ago. The unemployment rate, according to official figures, is 7 percent, but the actual figure is estimated to be between 10 and 12 percent. The difference between what could be produced and what is actually being produced in the United States, the most industrialized country in the world, amounts to some $200 billion a year—a loss of approximately $600 million per working day. Real wages are falling despite the fact that we have the means to increase them—that is, to increase purchasing power—by at least 3 to 4 percent a year.

2

On a Boat Without a Navigator

Statistics, however, do not reflect the entire situation. A whole generation is growing up under conditions of unemployment and hopelessness. The unemployment rate for teenagers is estimated to be over 20 percent. More than half of those graduating from college in 1976 either are without employment or are in jobs where they cannot make full use of their knowledge. This demoralizing and dehumanizing situation may have lasting effects.

We are told that one day the recession may bottom out and that in six to ten years the nation will again be producing at the level of a few years ago. This is possible, but all the suffering of the past few years will not be undone, and little assurance has been given that a new recession will not appear. Without major reforms in our economic policies, the potential for economic decline will be just as great as it is now, if not greater. Because of this threat, the majority of blue-collar and white-collar workers live in a situation of painful uncertainty.

Statistics show us that a recession is an economic crisis, but not that it is a social human crisis as well. This social and human crisis is not so easily passed. The fear and feeling of uncertainty, the psychology of recession, may remain and affect human and economic relationships deeply and permanently.

In addition, statistics do not express the anxiety that a world devoid of values or perspectives—a world without directions or goals—creates among people. Living in such a world is like taking a cruise on a boat without a navigator: we are all moving somewhere quickly, but no one seems to know our final destination.

The tragedy is that we have the potential to establish and achieve beneficial goals and directions. It is possible for us to create a world without unemployment, inflation, and recession, a world where the more developed nations can help the underdeveloped, and a world where we can all live in peace.

Science and Economics

Our economy is based on science. At the level of business enterprises—the microeconomic level—the production of goods and services (everything from grain to a pair of shoes, from mass transportation to the jumbo jets) has reached its present state of development because of applied science. In agriculture, for example, fertilizers, antibiotics, sophisticated machinery, and improved farming methods are scientific products that have increased output fifteen times per agricultural worker. Without applied science, we would revert to an underdeveloped nation. We would not be able to maintain our standard of living, or even to provide food for everyone. Most people in our society would be condemned to poverty and starvation.

What is true for the microeconomy is also true for the macroeconomy—the economy of the nation as a whole. It, too, is run by science. All highly developed societies—economists call them mature societies—have a great army of well-educated and intelligent economic thinkers at the governmental level who are deeply concerned with the fate of their nation's economy. An impressive sophistication and a tremendous scope of knowledge characterize the men and women who, through the science of economics, study and control the economies of their countries. And yet with all this scientific knowledge and technical sophistication we find ourselves in the midst of economic chaos. What could possibly have gone wrong?

Common-Sense Goals and Our Economic Challenge

There is no doubt that the governments, the economists, the businessmen, and particularly the ordinary person all wish

4

to have full employment, a stable currency, and an end to the tragic economic situation that plagues us. However, as we will explain, in the science of economics, there are no theories that accept even the possibility of full employment and a stable price level, no theories that have been conceived with a regard for the relation of human beings to the natural environment. Our scientific economic knowledge cannot even advise us how to orient the economy toward these goals.

It is because of these deficiencies in conventional economic thinking that our current economic situation seems so hopeless, and it is at this point that we must leave conventional economic theory behind. Full employment and stable purchasing power must be seen as the most natural and desirable economic situation. A human being's ability and desire to be a useful member of society, to earn a living, and to have the opportunity to produce goods and services needed by the community while respecting the natural environment must be regarded as basic preconditions for any society. A socioeconomic system that cannot make use of its potential to meet the needs of its citizens must be regarded as a system that is sick.

Unemployment should be considered not merely as a set of statistics but as a crime against humanity, depriving us of our basic right to lead a dignified life. An economic theory that justifies unemployment should consequently be regarded as a theory justifying crimes against humankind.

Theories justifying inflation are as immoral as those justifying unemployment. Inflation deprives people of what they should earn for their labor. It is a form of stealing, and the mere fact that it is justified theoretically and exists within a legal framework does not alter the fact that it, too, is a crime against humankind. A government that issues money which is losing its purchasing power has become, by this very fact, responsible for its society's lack of faith and for its growing sense of insecurity and hopelessness.

There is, finally, an issue that has come to the foreground

in the past twenty years—that of the environment. We can no longer afford to disregard the problems of increasingly limited natural resources and people's effect upon and relation to their natural environment.

Our current economic challenge is to solve the problems of full employment and stable purchasing power on the basis of ecological concerns. These are the most natural and basic goals—the common-sense goals of any socioeconomic system. Any society or nation that wishes to survive must accept the challenge of and responsibility for achieving these goals.

The Failure of Conventional Economics

Conventional economics does not, of course, accept these goals as its task; it does not even regard them as attainable. Because of this, nations that might wish to orient their economies toward these goals are at a loss. They don't know how to proceed or how to control their economies accordingly.

The idea that economics as a science and the economists who study it have not been concerned with achieving these goals must seem strange. What could economists and economics have been concerned with if not this task? How could economics have developed into a science and at the same time have refused to consider ways of reaching such basic and natural goals? It seems that these are questions anyone with common sense would have to ask. Why haven't our educated economists asked them?

This is the crux of the problem in economics today: Economics, as a science, has not heeded the wisdom of common sense. Human values and ideals have been excluded from conventional economic theory; the goals that are essential to the survival of human beings in a humanistic society have been ignored.

Where Economic Scientists Went Wrong

Conventional economic scientists apply the same scientific method as the natural scientists. They study the economy in the same way that natural scientists study nature. A physicist who observes the forces of atomic energy does just that: observing but not attempting to change that force; simply trying to discover how it works and to determine how it could be used. He or she is not supposed to think in terms of values, for the issue is not whether atomic energy in itself is good or bad; the primary goal is to determine its nature and its utility.

This is the same approach economists take toward the workings of an economic system. If an economist sees that unemployment and inflation occur together, he or she will be concerned with finding out the relationship between the two: In what ways and under what circumstances will inflation affect unemployment, and vice versa. The economist will be "scientific," and will express this relationship in mathematical language, just as the physicist does.

In aping natural scientists, the economists, in their desire to be exact, to be able to predict, to be objective and value-free, have been blinded to everything that cannot be exact, that cannot be quantified or predicted. They have excluded from their "science" any ideas, approaches, or goals that involve values or subjective interpretations. In order to do this, these "scientific" economists have closed their eyes to the fact that the subject of their studies—the economy—is essentially different from what is studied by a physicist or some other natural scientist.

Unlike nature, the economy does not exist independently of human beings; it is their creation. That economy is a product of human beings and their society, that it came about in the process of developing the ability to think, that the human dimension, which is so essential to economics, cannot be quantified, that human behavior cannot be predicted, and that human relationships cannot be expressed in exact terms and concepts —all this that common sense reveals has been forgotten or ignored by those who have developed the science of economics.

The reader may be interested to know that one of the authors of this book was once an ardent advocate of Marxism and the planned economy; he was involved in the planning of the national economy of Czechoslovakia. At the same time, he was determined to be a humanist, and it took him a long time to realize the incompatibility of his two beliefs. Eventually, he found that, like other planners, he, too, thought only in terms of target figures, and the humanism that he felt would be an automatic by-product of the system was slowly being destroyed by it. For him, as well, humankind had become a specific concern only after "working hours."

Changing Our Economic Orientation

The first step in a common-sense approach to economics is that the economy must be seen as *a system of human beings* —human beings who think, work, invent, organize, and design, individuals who have spiritual and emotional desires and expectations. Consequently, economics must begin to incorporate these varied emotions, abilities, ambitions, expectations, dreams, and frustrations into its theories and concepts. These new components are obviously nonquantifiable, and, as such, are not "scientific," yet they are the decisive components in our lives and in the economy.

Further, although conventional economics, like the natural sciences, claims to be value-free, it should be clear from what we have said that any science dealing with human beings must be based on *human values,* and must *not* be value-free. Conventional economics sees in the economy a relationship of commodities; anybody who perceives the economy with common sense regards it as a relationship among human beings. While conventional economists have eliminated the human element from their theories, we shall put it into the center of ours.

The basic difference between conventional and human-centered economics is that the first is theoretically based on exact and objective science, while the second is based on human values. More important, however, is the difference between the utility of the two approaches.

Conventional economists regard economic phenomena in much the same way as, say, a meteorologist regards the weather: Inflation and recession or economic booms are "natural" phenomena, as are hurricanes and sunshine; nothing can be done either to prevent or to foster their occurrence. The role of the conventional economist is thus simply to study the past and predict the future.

In contrast, common sense requires that economists see unemployment and inflation as situations to be avoided and an economic boom as a natural and achievable goal. Our view is that the true role of the economist is to study the past in order to *create* the future of our economy.

The Individual's Role and the Power of "Common Sense"

No doubt the reader feels that this new approach to economics is idealistic but not particularly practical. Faced with the complicated problems of a mature society and the powerful vested interests that control it, what can an individual armed only with common sense possibly hope to achieve? The thousands of learned economists who deal with economic problems have developed a language all their own; their theories can be judged only by other members of their field. How could an individual, or even a group of concerned employees or consumers, prove the sophisticated economists wrong? And if they could, what alternatives could they offer?

9

These doubts are valid ones, but the power of common sense—the intellectual and moral strength of even the most unskilled laborers—should not be underestimated. The role of common sense in the development of the contemporary economy is actually far greater than is generally recognized. It did, in fact, have a hand in upsetting the theories of two of the greatest and most influential economic thinkers of the 19th century—David Ricardo* and Karl Marx.

Both Ricardo and Marx claimed that the reward, or wage, given to workers must remain at the subsistence level. Ricardo felt that if the supply of labor was higher than the demand for it, wages, adhering to the law of supply and demand, would fall under the subsistence level. This would lead to a decline in the number of available workers. When the supply of labor fell below the demand, according to the law, wages would again increase. This would, in turn, lead to an increase in the labor force, the cycle would repeat itself, and wages would fluctuate at or around the subsistence level. Maintaining wages at this level in the first place would eliminate wild swings in the employment level and result in a more stable economy. According to Ricardo's theory, there was no one to blame for this unfortunate situation; it was simply an economic law that, like any natural law, must be accepted.

Marx acknowledged the existence of universal or natural economic laws and agreed with Ricardo's theory of subsistence wages. He maintained, however, that this theory was valid only in the capitalist system. Once private ownership was eliminated and capitalism was transcended, this law would disappear, along with the system that supported it.

The followers of Marx also felt that the laws could not

---

* The Englishman David Ricardo, while less well known to the general public than Marx, is accepted by experts as the most important theoretician of the classical school of capitalism in the 19th century.

be changed, and hence, for them, the only reasonable way to improve conditions for the workers was to abolish capitalism.

The Triumph of the Ordinary Person

Yet those who were the most affected by these "iron-clad" laws—the workers themselves—reacted quite differently from the rest. They refused to be ruled by theoretical laws and began to fight for an improvement in their hard and inhuman way of life. The pressure they were able to put on those who owned the means of production eventually resulted in a search for solutions to the problems of low wages and poor working conditions. The solutions themselves involved the transcendence of these "economic laws."

Innovations included more efficient ways of organizing the workers in the shops and advanced technology that made it possible for more goods to be produced with less effort. As the production process was based on a higher level of thinking, and as science and technology developed further, the demands of both the capitalists and the workers could be met. In this way, the human element—common sense—celebrated its first victory over economic theories.

Common Sense Must Triumph Again

Although our description is a simplification, it does illustrate the failure of economics to use common sense and to consider the importance of the human element and the ability to think, whether in day-to-day living or, at a higher level, the ability to think scientifically. Of course, the application of science, through advanced technology, to the production process was not caused solely by the economic and political pressure exerted by the workers, but they did have a tremendous impact on the development of this application of science.

From all of this, it should be clear that common sense is a factor to be reckoned with in economic change, even though that reckoning will not be easy. We cannot let the "laws" and theories of sophisticated economists force us into a passive acceptance of our economic problems.

Naturally, the problems of today are far more complicated than those of the past century. Simply applying pressure for change—by means of a strike, for example—will not solve anything. New ways of bringing about economic change must be used in dealing with the new and unfamiliar wave of economic problems.

Allaying the Crisis: Knowledge Means Power

As a first step in moving away from our current economic crisis, people must come to realize that our economic difficulties are not simply those of one class or group. Inflation, unemployment, and an endangered environment affect not just blue-collar workers or environmentalists but the nation and, in fact, the world as a whole.

Coupled with an awareness of the magnitude of the problem is the importance of knowing its causes and how to deal with them. In the early stages of the workers' movement in Europe in the late 19th century, the slogan "Knowledge means power" symbolized a significant factor in this movement. Understanding the workings of the social and economic processes at that time became an important intellectual tool in making the workers' movement a powerful political force. The magnitude of the problems that confront us today makes it imperative that the person in the street, the person with common sense, the majority of the nation rather than a small minority, should become aware of where the roots of the problems lie and how to fight them. It is the task of this book to show how to change the trends of our social system toward a brighter economic future.

The Scapegoats

When we try to determine the roots of our economic evils, common sense can prevent us from relying on conventional and simplistic answers. Traditionally, all our economic ills have been attributed to the presumed evil nature of human beings, or to the form of ownership of the means of production. While these causes may have been valid at one time, the mature economy is far too complex a system for changes in either of these two areas to have any great effect.

In the so-called capitalist countries, most often it was privately owned big business that received all the criticism in times of economic distress. Big business increased prices, it fired employees, it polluted; these were, and still are, some of the more common complaints against economic systems based on private ownership. Yet it should be remembered that social systems with *no* private ownership have existed for decades, and their economic problems arc much worse than ours. In socialist or communist countries, the prices are higher, the quality of goods is far inferior, unemployment is exchanged for forced labor, and environmental concern is minimal. While Western consumers have limited consumer rights, there are practically no consumer rights in the planned economy of the Soviet model. The consumer may buy only what has been produced according to the target figures of the national economic plan.

As an alternative to the private ownership of the West and the state ownership of the Soviet Union, a third type of ownership, in which the workers own and operate the means of production, has been introduced in Yugoslavia. Yet Yugoslavia has one of the highest rates of inflation in Europe, and the unemployment rate is so high that many Yugoslavs have been forced to work in other countries. If these workers lose their jobs and have to return home, a major economic catastrophe can be expected in Yugoslavia.

Changing the Form of Ownership

Actually, it is a great pity that we cannot change the performance of the economic system simply by changing the form of ownership or by passing some "progressive" and far-reaching legislation. If only a new era of full employment, no inflation, and effective environmental protection could result from simply passing some new laws! Unfortunately, experience has shown us that this is not possible. For instance, the employment act passed by the United States Congress in 1946 made the government responsible for guaranteeing nearly full employment and a stable currency. However, it's clear that this law had little or no effect. In such a complex economy, mere legislative measures are worthless. The economy is not simply the relationship of different commodities to one another guided by abstract "economic laws," or that between large corporations and consumers; it is a relationship of human beings, and this type of relationship is not changed simply by introducing new laws or new forms of ownership.

Changing Human Nature

Many philosophers and other social critics point to human nature as the main cause of our social and economic ills. They assume that if everyone acted reasonably, if everyone behaved with the goodness and the honesty that are inherent in all of us, the world would be a better place, and we would not face the crisis that we do.

There is no doubt that such a state of affairs would be more than desirable and that it would improve life for everyone, yet we must question the practicality of such a solution. Even if people did behave in such a noble manner, the changes needed are too great and time is too short to put all our faith in simple answers. In addition, human beings have many shortcomings and don't always behave nobly. There is also the question whether such an improvement would affect the economy in the ways we would intend it to. Would reasonable human beings necessarily create an economy without inflation or unemployment?

Reasonable Actions, Unreasonable Results

Despite the efforts of both individuals and businesses to act in a reasonable manner, the economy is such that more often than not it would react quite unreasonably. For example, it would be reasonable and beneficial for both a corporation and for the economy as a whole if the corporation increased productivity. The usual way to do this is to replace employees with machines. Yet the unemployment that would result is both unreasonable and inhuman. Similarly, it would be reasonable for an enterprise to project a wage increase into a price increase for its products, but the effect of this measure, inflation, is also both unreasonable and undesirable.

In the 18th century, the Scottish economist Adam Smith —the founder of capitalist theory—assumed that an "invisible hand" was guiding the economy in such a way that the "selfish" and "unreasonable" acts of those involved would, in the end, create a reasonable and beneficial economic situation. As economics progressed from a field of study to a science, the ideas and concepts of its theorists were given scientific credibility and were termed "laws." These laws were once effective in helping the economists watch over and predict the minor fluctuations in a smoothly running economy. They also served to justify and strengthen whatever economic behavior they applied to; under the law of the invisible hand, men were permitted to be unreasonable, for the theory stated that their acts would have beneficial consequences.

Today, however, our economists have found that the economy has outgrown its old laws. Now the invisible hand seems to be working in reverse, creating *chaos* out of the *reasonable actions* of today's economic actors. The corporations are run by experts, but their actions more often than not create our economic malaise, and the economic theories only justify the process. In this way, unemployment and inflation are theoretically and scientifically explained and justified like any natural catastrophe. They have become, because of these new theories, justified and inevitable, as has the failure of our economists to deal with them effectively.

In December of 1974, at the convention of the American Economic Association, Professor Walter Heller, the Association's chairman and former economic adviser to President Johnson, gave a lecture on "What Is Good with Economics." In his lecture, he made this statement:

> For some thirty years, we have warned that full employment, price stability, and full freedom of economic choice cannot co-exist in a world of strongly organized producer groups. More recently, economic analysis has brought home the unromantic truth that failure to cure some of our social ills traces less to a failure of will, or "right-wing villains" or a calloused "establishment" or *powerlessness of the people* than to the prosaic facts that the problems are tough and complex, the goals we seek may be irreconcilable—in short, traces more to conflicts in our national objectives than to conflicts among social groups.

As this statement suggests, for a whole generation economists were concerned not so much with creating a social order of full employment, price stability, and full freedom of economic choice, as with justifying the opposite course. They spread a theory that, once accepted, became a self-fulfilling prophecy.

Powerful People With Visible Hands

The words "powerlessness of the people" were emphasized by Mr. Heller in his statement. The people of the world will be powerless in the face of economic disaster if they continue to accept the wisdom of their economic scientists. A powerless public accepting the economists' "laws" will permit those laws to "act," and we will find not only that full employment and a stable currency will cease to exist but also that even our civilization may cease to exist.

We have already shown how the workers, the public, prevailed with their common sense over the theories of the great economic thinkers Ricardo and Marx. Should it not be possible to achieve the same victory over their less-gifted pupils? The "powerlessness of the people" in this context refers simply to a belief: Those who believe that it is in their power to change the catastrophic state of affairs are no longer powerless. This belief can be fostered only by our understanding of the economy we live in.

Belief and understanding will, of course, not be sufficient for change. An awareness and knowledge of *how* to bring about change is important. With this knowledge, we can and must change the orientation of our socioeconomic order. We have the power to become the "visible hands" that will redirect it away from the abyss and orient it toward healthy and humane goals.

We see the purpose of this book as helping to find the road to a society where unemployment, inflation, and ecological disharmony will, for all practical purposes, be eliminated; where the nation as a whole will share the wealth we are able to create. We realize that "man does not live by bread alone," and therefore not only our point of departure but all the stages of our thought will respect the spiritual, moral, and ethical values of humanity, and we shall deal with the economic problems and solutions with this understanding.

A Revolution in Our Minds, Not in the Streets

Thus, we invite all who are interested in or dedicated to a humane social system to follow the road to a revolution in our minds, to a revolutionary rethinking of terms, concepts, and methods that have long been taken for granted. The major economic revolutions—the industrial, postindustrial, scientific, and technological—have been completed. The spiritual revolution, that must happen in our minds rather than in the streets, is the next great historical step to be taken.

If we want to change our economy, we must know what we are changing and what kinds of changes we should make. It is from this angle that we will attempt to explain what the essence of today's economy is and, consequently, what kind of economics would be a viable tool to perform the changes.

2

The Essence of Economy and the Fallacies of Conventional Economics

Humans and Nature

The relationship between humans and nature is inherently one of conflict. As human beings, we all have a great desire to live, yet, as part of nature, we are mortal and doomed to die. We are dependent upon nature for the food necessary to sustain life; we are responsible for obtaining it in sufficient quantity, and this is often no easy task. Further, although we have been given life and the instinct for survival, as one of the more fragile creatures of the earth, we find that there is much in nature which threatens our existence, and from which we must constantly protect ourselves. We are part of nature and at the same time dependent upon it; we rely on that part of it which gives life and fear that part of it which can take it away.

These things are true for all the creatures of this earth. Human beings, however, have something that places us above the others: We are endowed with the ability to be aware of our conflict with nature and to overcome it. We are able to bring into the disharmony between ourselves and nature a harmony of our own.

This ability is the one that enables us to think and to feel, to be not only a physiological entity but a spiritual one as well. Through this ability, we have attempted to make ourselves less dependent on nature and to greatly reduce the threat to our existence. We have given ourselves more freedom and have become our own master. Because our physiological and spiritual nature makes us unique in the world, we can decide whether our spiritual nature will guide us and make us more creatures of reason and common sense or whether our physiological nature will force us to give in to the whims of nature as any other animal would do.

20

Philosophical Roots and Economic Philosophy

These ideas concerning humans and their relationship to nature originate in the Judeo-Christian philosophy, which tells us that our dependence upon nature and our ability to overcome it have existed since the beginning of time, when God first created humans, infused them with a soul, or spirit, and created nature for their use. It is the soul, the creative ability, that separates humans from the rest of nature and, at the same time, enables them to resolve their conflicts with and eliminate their dependence upon nature.

It is our belief that an awareness of the influence of the Judeo-Christian philosophy on Western civilization lends itself to a clearer and more accurate understanding of the success and the failure of our society and culture. It is through this perspective, what we call the perspective of common sense, that our society, and particularly our economy, shall be interpreted.

With regard to the economic crisis currently confronting Western society, it is important to realize that the philosophies of the two main economic systems of Western culture *deviate* from the Judeo-Christian tradition. Although Adam Smith was a moral philosopher and an ardent Christian, he developed an economic philosophy, with its "invisible hand," that justified selfish and unreasonable behavior on the part of the economic actors and took the control of the economy away from the ordinary person. Those tenets of the Judeo-Christian philosophy which emphasized human creative ability and the commitment to love one's neighbor, fully recognized by Smith the philosopher and human being, were neglected by Smith the economist.

Similarly, Karl Marx, in his philosophical manuscripts, often referred to people as creative beings, and yet as a social scientist he undermined this creative potential through his ideas concerning a human being's relationship to nature and to other humans. Marx assumed that this relationship was one in which humanity and nature equally contribute to each other's development. Marx ignored the spiritual part of human beings and viewed the history of humankind as a natural process: people and society develop according to laws equally valid for human and nature. Both Marx and Smith developed economic theories in which people's ability to control economy and society had no place. Both of these men—the one on the right and the one on the left, one a Christian and the other a Jew—ignored human creative capability for making use of the forces of nature. They ignored the fact that human beings may be just cogs in the economic system but are also its shapers. Consequently, human beings are responsible for the behavior of the economy, and we are therefore responsible for the humane or antihumane direction of the economy. In the failure of Smith and Marx, we find the philosophical roots of our current economic crisis.

Economy as a Creation of Thinking

The desire of humans to live a free and dignified life has manifested itself through work, both physical and intellectual. The ability to think has allowed them to discover and use the natural forces that surround them. Mechanical forces, like those found in the flow of water or in wind; chemical forces, such as fire; biochemical forces, such as those used to grow food—all have been discovered, harnessed, and put to humanity's use.

Today, we are at that stage of human development where the ability to think has produced the highly sophisticated natural sciences that underlie the process of changing natural wealth into human wealth. This process is the essence of economy.

Economy is essentially the transformation of natural forces and natural goods into forces and goods that serve humanity. It is an order created by thinking people, and one that has developed as a result of people's intellectual and spiritual growth. Further, it should be clear that when we regard economy as the creation of thinking human beings, economic wealth becomes nothing more than the transformation of natural wealth. There is no material wealth except that of nature and that created by humans from nature.

Economy, Spirit, and Intellect

Certainly, human spiritual and intellectual ability has not been confined to solving our conflict with nature or focused solely on the transformation process that we call economy. It has also discovered the beauty in nature and developed an admiration and love for it. Human beings have always been concerned with nature's mysteries, the secret of the atom and of life and death, and this spirit has tried to encompass physics and metaphysics in order to transcend these limitations with the strength of intellect. From the most primitive thinking in the cradle of civilization to today's complex technological theories and concepts, an endless stream of thoughts and ideas, all manifestations of humanity's spirit, whether in philosophy, science, or the arts, has created the cultural continuum. In dealing with economics, we should be aware of the existence of this continuum and of the fact that our economic thinking is but a small and so far inglorious part of it.

This concept is an important one, for it underlies the idea that the transformation process, or economy, is a *part* of the life of the nations of this earth, a part of human society and the human beings who make it up. As human knowledge has grown, so economy grew, and the transformation process was elevated from the most primitive levels of hunting and farming to the complex and scientifically based economy of today. In the same way that economic thinking cannot be isolated from the cultural continuum, it also cannot be isolated from the entire cultural, intellectual, and spiritual life of contemporary society. As soon as people forget about all this, they lose perspective, and become selfish and victims of their own negative qualities.

A Successful Economy?

With this concept of economy in mind, we must now seriously question whether or not we have achieved the harmony we mentioned earlier. Did we really achieve the harmony between humans and nature, and between human beings, that we have sought? Unfortunately, it is obvious that we did not. Why? Why did we create conditions that have increased our dependence on nature and its resources instead of eliminating it? Instead of making nature serve us, why do we suddenly find ourselves about to destroy it, and, in doing so, to destroy ourselves? Why has economy become a machine that rules over people instead of serving them? One answer is that humans have lost perspective and have applied a selfish approach to solving problems—thinking, for instance, only in terms of power, profits or other benefits. The harmony we seek, however, can be found only when we understand that rights flow from responsibility. Human beings must use their intellectual, spiritual, and moral awareness to keep themselves conscious of their duties toward other human beings and the environment in which they live.

Another obvious answer might be that there are powerful vested interests, institutions, and groups that benefit from our present situation and have the power to maintain it and even to develop it further. But such an answer is too simple. It focuses on the consequences of the failure of economy but not its causes, on certain features of the problem but not on its essence.

The Kingdom of Commodities

Regardless of the subjective or psychological motivations behind our current crisis, what has actually happened is that *we have forgotten people and their desire for freedom.* We have forgotten that the great gift which distinguishes human beings from all other creatures in the world is the ability to think and that this ability gives us the power to change our relationship to nature and to create a "Kingdom of God" on nature's imperfect earth. Instead, we have created a "Kingdom of Commodities," whose leaders and rulers became those who possess and control these commodities.

In order to better understand this problem, let us compare our interpretation of economy as the creation of human genius, the common-sense approach, with the generally accepted definition of contemporary economics and the economy. This definition is taken from the internationally famous and widely used college textbook *Economics,* by Paul Samuelson:

> Economists today agree on a general definition something like the following: Economics is the study of how men and society end up *choosing,* with or without the use of money, to employ *scarce* resources which could have alternative uses, to produce various commodities and distribute them for consumption, now or in the future, among various people and groups in society.*

The oversimplification and consequent fallacy of such definitions can be easily demonstrated.

The Philosophy of the Bookkeeper

To prove our point, let us take as an example the art of cooking as it applies to the restaurant business. The master

---

* Paul A. Samuelson, *Economics,* McGraw-Hill Book Company, eighth ed., p. 4.

chef possesses the remarkable gift of knowing how to combine and process many different ingredients to create a menu that will delight our senses as well as our appetites. This combination of imagination, craftsmanship, and art, which must satisfy the discriminating gourmet, would be defined, according to our economists, as an allocation of "scarce resources which could have alternative uses, to produce various commodities. . . ."

We could imagine that the bookkeeper of a restaurant would accept such a definition. Professional interest lies in quantifying what materials have been purchased, how much they have cost, and in what ways and for how much profit they have been sold to the public. The taste and ability of the chef and the expectations and satisfactions of the customers cannot be part of the bookkeeping entries and are not really of any concern. Yet these nonquantifiable elements of cooking and eating are the more important ones. As a consumer, our bookkeeper would in fact be very much concerned with them when trying to decide where to dine out.

This is not intended to be a criticism of bookkeeping, for there is nothing wrong with that approach to cooking or to any other economic activity. After all, bookkeeping is an integral part of our economy, and it would not be an exaggeration to state that without proper bookkeeping our mature economy would disappear as quickly as it would without, say, energy. The problems begin when bookkeeping and the thinking behind it are applied to areas where they have no relevance.

The point is that the application of the method of thinking which underlies Samuelson's definition has forced conventional economics to reduce the economy to allocation, to what is easily quantifiable: Everything that is not quantifiable has been eliminated. While our common-sense approach focuses on the transformation process and can incorporate the full range of factors essential to any economy, *conven-*

tional economics has actually been reduced to a kind of book-keeping dealing only with things that can be put into numbers. To clarify our point, let us use a second example—the production of a car.

Production Is More Than Allocation

We could look at the production of an automobile as simply the allocation of materials for, and the assembly of, a large number of parts, each of them needing some scarce resource to be constructed on its own. Yet we must question whether it means anything at all to perceive automobile production in this way. Looking at the economics of automobile production in terms of human creative ability, we can see that it involves much more than simply "allocation and assembly."

Behind the invention of the automobile lies the discovery that crude oil, if processed, will explode under certain conditions—that burning it frees a tremendous amount of energy. With this discovery came a question: Would it be possible to control this energy and put it to humanity's use? Something had to be developed that would *transform this natural force into a productive one.*

For decades, scientists worked to create such a transformer. In time, they learned how to process crude oil into gasoline; an engine was invented, along with the many different parts necessary for its proper and efficient functioning; electrical systems and tires were designed, tested, and improved; special steel and cast-iron products were invented and applied to car production, along with special glass, fabrics, paints, and other materials. Behind all this were developments in the chemical industry, the mining industry, the machine-tool industry, and the electric industry, and from it and alongside it grew large factories, a banking industry, improved transportation and communications systems, and a great number of research institutes. The basis of it all was the educational system, without which no administrator, designer, automotive specialist, or bookkeeper could exist.

Essentials Cannot Be Quantified

Of course, "scarce resources" had to be allocated as well. Designers had to take into consideration what materials were available and whether they could be used. In most cases, however, special materials were needed and had to be invented. It is important to realize that the *allocation of scarce resources* is the end, rather than the beginning, of a designer's work.

Thus, through the perspective that common sense gives us, an automobile is not simply the collection and assembly of different parts or the allocation of scarce resources. It is the product of a whole army of highly educated, specially trained, gifted, and creative people (and the institutions and organizations behind them) who first designed the car and then requested the material to build it. The allocation of resources is a part of this process, and it happens that this part can be quantified, but the genius of the inventors, designers, scientists, and administrators and all the other intangible but essential elements of automobile production cannot.

Our bookkeeper will, of course, deal only with what the principles of bookkeeping require, the quantifiable parts, the figures. Yet what kind of entry shall note the ability of human beings to think and to create, the commitment to one's work, the initiative, creativity, and other essential elements out of which the modern car emerged? The bookkeeper has no use for these common-sense elements. He or she may be well aware of all that we have said, but *the system of bookkeeping is such that he or she can register only what is quantifiable and not necessarily what is essential.*

The "Scientific" Economist

The same is true for the conventional economist. Of course, he or she is a person with common sense, and so is aware of what we are saying here. But the human elements in the economics of car production cannot be put into figures. How can they? How can economists be "exact scientists" if they force themselves to deal with such elements as thought, creativity, and initiative?

The answer is that they can't. Conventional economists believe that, as scientists, they have to eliminate all of these common-sense essentials. In their world of equations, definitional statements, and graphs, whatever cannot be quantified has no place. Human beings can enter this world only as statistics; no human quality can be considered.

It makes no difference to our bookkeeper whether he or she is dealing with the production of horse-drawn carts two hundred years ago or the production of an automobile today. The terms of reference are still the hours of labor spent and the amount of scarce resources used; only the figures and the number of entries will change. The same is true for economists who use the definition we have quoted above. The fact that the cart was produced in a relatively primitive economy based primarily on empirical knowledge while the car is produced in an economy based on highly developed and sophisticated scientific technology makes no difference to them. The many changes that have had to occur in the development from cart to automobile production cannot be worked into this scientific definition of economics and are simply ignored.

The "Scientific Method" and Its Consequences

It is obvious that there is a great difference between the production of a car and a cart, and that today's mature economy resembles the economy of two hundred years ago only in name. Yet the "science" of economics, according to its definition, remains the same; it does not account for the tremendous differences between that time and our own. The economist who is faithful to Samuelson's definition and, as such, is faithful to the scientific method of the natural sciences becomes divorced from the true nature of the contemporary economy and does not consider the revolutionary changes that have taken place in the two hundred years since Adam Smith wrote his *Wealth of Nations* or in the hundred years since Marx wrote his *Capital*.

In this, we can clearly see the difference between common sense and the so-called scientific approach and realize the unfortunate consequences of the latter. The scientific approach is not concerned with the reality of the situation or with the differences between economies today and those of the past. Instead, it focuses on the reduction of complex occurrences to some common, but often meaningless, similarities. It is through this method that economists have tried to become as exact and scientific as the natural scientists are. The approach has added more scientific credibility and respect to the field, but because of it economics is forced to ignore the important human elements of the economy and so loses its effectiveness in dealing with our economic problems.

When this method is applied to economics, we call it reductionist, because it results in the reduction of a complex economy to a few simple components. We could also call it a mechanical method, because it refers to the separate components of the economy as if they were part of a mechanical system rather than part of a system of thinking human beings.

Unchanging "Laws" for a Changing Economy

Natural scientists assume that whatever happens in nature has to happen: Natural phenomena do not occur by accident; they are the product of some cause or force that, once understood, can be formulated as a natural law. This assumption is an essential part of the natural sciences; without it, they could not have developed the theories and principles that are so important to us today.

As an example, let us consider the frequently observed phenomenon of a stone or any other object falling to the ground. Because we assume that stones *have* to fall to the ground—that falling is the product of some consistent and reliable force rather than an accident—we have been able to derive a natural law, the law of gravity, to explain this force and its effects. The science of physics uses this law in predicting the behavior of similar objects and in many other related areas.

Conventional economists, in trying to emulate the natural scientists, also assume, in formulating their economic theories, that certain natural laws are at work. They have observed, for instance, that there is statistical evidence of a parallel growth of the money supply and the prices of products, and have simply assumed that this relationship is an inevitable and permanent one. Theories and economic laws are then derived from this assumption to explain and define how the quantity of money is responsible for the level of prices in an economic system.

Conventional economists have failed to realize that the economy is far too complex for such a simplistic assumption. To reduce the multitude of components and an endless number of relationships to only two or three for the purpose of developing useful and explanatory theories and laws is neither justified by nor relevant to scientific thinking. As a creation of thinking human beings, a system such as our economy is growing and changing just as fast as the level of this thinking. To assume that any relationship between two or three components will be constant and unchanging in the future simply because it has been so for a few decades is both fallacious and unscientific. This kind of assumption will inevitably lead to most ineffective and damaging theories and concepts.

The Abyss Between Economics and Economy

As long as we continue to see the economy as merely the allocation of scarce resources and apply methods of studying it that are reductionist and mechanistic, economics will remain a sophisticated form of bookkeeping and never become a tool that can be instrumental in helping us solve our economic problems. By using a natural-science approach to a social-science subject, we lose the economic reality, and economics develops into a pseudo-science.

But by regarding the economy as a system created by thinking human beings we shall begin to focus on *why* our economy works the way it does rather than *how*. In this way, having seen that this system is not working according to our expectations, we can concern ourselves with the mistakes we have made, and, at the same time, use this new understanding to *create* scientific tools that will help us to *redirect* our economy toward the *goals* we have chosen.

With this in mind, we can return to the question we posited earlier: Why is it that our economy is about to control us instead of serving us? Our new understanding of economy and economics will bring us closer to the answer.

Confusing the Means With the End

To begin with, we have forgotten that science is merely a tool, and one that can be used to achieve humane goals for human beings and their society. Fascinated by what science achieved for us, we began to feel that science is an end itself, and would reduce our dependence on nature and solve all our economic problems. Instead, we should have oriented our thinking toward the ways in which applied science, or technology, could be used not only to make us less dependent upon nature but also, and more important, to make us freer citizens who are not ruled by technology, bureaucracy, or power interests.

32

Economics as a Tool to Mold Our Future

In order to change this unfortunate turn of events, we must begin to revolutionize our thinking about our world and our economic concepts. The first step is to *stop regarding the economy simply as the allocation of scarce resources* and economics as the science that studies this process. Instead, we should see the *economy as man's attempt to become independent of nature in order to make himself a freer and more independent being.* Economics should come to be seen as *the study of what measures should be taken in order to make the economy serve humanity in this way.* Certain goals must be chosen, by the majority of the nation rather than an elite and powerful few (whether they are politicians, corporate executives, or union leaders), and economics should become the tool to develop the ways in which our economy can be reoriented toward the achievement of these goals.

There is little doubt that, at least for the present, the basic, common-sense goals for any nation will be those of full employment, a stable currency, and ecological equilibrium. We should be aware that there are many roads to these goals. Full employment could be achieved under conditions of modern slavery and concentration camps, stable purchasing power on the basis of poverty, and ecological equilibrium through the elimination of modern technology. Thus, the goals themselves are not sufficient. *Economics must become a tool that will help free nations direct their economies toward goals decided upon within the framework of democracy and freedom.*

The Forgotten Words of Adam Smith

Two hundred years ago, Adam Smith revolutionized economic thinking by formulating the task of a political economy as that of providing scientific advice to the legislators on how to provide "plentiful revenue for the people." Much has happened since that time, and we must now regard Smith's definition of economics as too narrow. Yet the essence of his definition is far more rational today than that of the "allocation of scarce resources" used by our contemporaries.

More than providing "plentiful revenue," economics must now become the science that enriches political democracy by adding economic democracy. Economics must become the scientific tool through which the nation as a whole can decide its economic future, and that can offer democratic governments an instrument through which economic democracy can be realized.

Castles Made of Sand

In this chapter, we have tried to show that the development of Western civilization has its philosophical roots in the Judeo-Christian concept of humans and their relationship to nature. What we have called common sense is actually the application of this philosophy to everyday life. In particular, we have tried to prove that the decline of our civilization, characterized by our current economic crisis, is the result of a deviation from this philosophy, in which the role of humans as creative beings has been neglected.

Humans have built a sophisticated discipline, that of the social sciences, which has virtually done away with such basic ideals as one's love for a fellow human. In this, all that makes us human has been eliminated. For this reason, the intellectual foundations of this discipline, and the culture from which it developed, are made of sand and have begun to disintegrate. We have forgotten that human beings do not live by bread alone. We have forgotten the spiritual and moral part of the human being and developed society without the proper balance between humans and nature. We believe that the time has come for us to begin to rebuild these foundations, using the concept of humanity inherent in the Judeo-Christian philosophy as a guide.

It is from this angle that we shall interpret the great economic revolutions which have brought us to our present stage of economic development. This interpretation will give us a greater understanding of the problems we are facing and so enable us to shape our economic future. Particularly, we will be aware that all economic revolutions were revolutions in our ability to think, revolutions that did not occur on barricades, yet were revolutions that basically changed the world.

This understanding should encourage us to see that the revolution of our inhumane and crisis-driven economy to a just and plentiful economy requires a revolution in thinking, and not mindless repetitions of centuries-old theories and pseudorevolutionary slogans.

3
The Industrial Revolution

Simply a Revolution in Industry?

Almost everyone is aware of the term "Industrial Revolution," and most of us know that it refers to a period in history generally characterized by extensive mechanization and a shift from home manufacturing to large-scale factory production. When one considers that during this time, with the emergence of new social classes—the working and capitalist classes—and the resulting new social and economic relationships, the entire structure of society was reorganized, it does seem appropriate to call this period and its effects revolutionary. As a matter of fact, it was this revolution in industry that brought humankind to its present stage of social and economic development.

Because of this, we feel that in order to better understand our own economy it is necessary to understand what actually happened during the Industrial Revolution. Was it simply a mechanization and shift toward large-scale factory production, a *mere* "industrial revolution," or was it more?

Revolution as a Process

A political revolution like the French Revolution of 1789 or the October Revolution of 1917 in the Soviet Union is connected with exact dates. (We know the year, the month, and even the day when the most dramatic event in the course of supplanting one ruling body with another took place.) We may object to such simplifications of history, but this is not our concern at present. We are concerned with a socioeconomic revolution, the industrial one, and we do not find a day, a month, or even a decade to which it has been fixed.

The Industrial Revolution is said to have occurred during the second half of the 18th century in England, the leading industrial country of that century. Yet the roots of this revolution can be traced to at least the early Renaissance. We could go back to Roger Bacon or Copernicus, to the Crusades, to the Reformation or the Enlightenment, and find remarkable revolutionary new philosophies, works of art, and religious views, evidence of the impact of the political revolution in England in 1640—all of which laid the groundwork for the events and changes we are discussing.

This fact brings out an important characteristic of the Industrial Revolution and others like it: The "revolution" we are dealing with is *more a process than an event*. It did not involve people with revolutionary intentions or ambitions; our 18th-century counterparts were not even conscious of being subjects—or objects, for that matter—of the revolutionary changes that were taking place. These changes had an evolutionary character; they developed gradually and at different times.

The Need for a Revolution in Thought

Revolutions of this type are often so subtle that it is understandably difficult for those involved in them to discern the similarities and differences between the old and new worlds and, hence, to be conscious of the fact that a new and different socioeconomic system is being established. Once people discover these differences, however, once they become conscious of them, they can begin to support—or undermine —the new elements; they have a goal and can begin to work toward its achievement. This is an important element in widespread revolutionary change: *only when the reality of a social revolution has been grasped through a revolution in thinking can the social revolution go forward with all due speed.*

In regard to the Industrial Revolution, we must repeat that its roots are to be found in the great revolutions of thought that preceded it; they created an intellectual environment in which a new socioeconomic system could begin to develop. Equally important, however, is the fact that the continued growth and final maturation of this system depended on the degree to which it was "discovered" and understood by those who created it and were affected by it.

Adam Smith and the Division of Labor

The genius of Adam Smith was responsible for the "discovery" of the Industrial Revolution; Smith was the one who identified the elements that distinguished the new order from the old one. He saw the *division of labor* as the key to this new system, and developed an economic philosophy around it. His *Wealth of Nations,* published in 1776, described this new philosophy and quickly became established as the "Classic of Capitalism." Smith interprets the essence of the new system, the division of labor, this way:

"The greatest improvement in the productive powers of labor, and the greater part of the skill, dexterity, and judgment with which it is any where directed or applied, seem to have been the effects of the division of labor.

"The effects of the division of labor, in the general business of society, will be more easily understood, by considering in what manner it operates in some particular manufactures. It is commonly supposed to be carried furthest in some very trifling ones; not perhaps that it really is carried further in them than in others of more importance; but in those trifling manufactures which are destined to supply the small wants of but a small number of people, the whole number of workmen must necessarily be small; and those employed in every different branch of the work can often be collected into the same workhouse, and placed at once under the view of the spectator. In those great manufactures, on the contrary, which are destined to supply the great wants of the great body of the people, every different branch of the work employs so great a number of workmen, that it is impossible to collect them all into the same workhouse. We can seldom see more, at one time, than those employed in one single branch. Though in such manufactures, therefore, the work may really be divided into a much greater number of parts, than in those of a more trifling nature, the division is not near so obvious, and has accordingly been much less observed.

"To take an example, therefore, from a very trifling manufacture; but one in which the division of labor has been very often taken notice of, the trade of the pinmaker; a workman not educated to this business (which the division of labor has rendered a distinct trade), nor acquainted with the use of the machinery employed in it (to the invention of which the same division of labor has probably given occasion), could scarce, perhaps, with his utmost industry, make one pin in a day, and certainly could not make twenty. But in the way in which this business is now carried on, not only the whole work is a particular trade, but it is divided into a number of branches, of which the greater part are likewise peculiar trades. One man draws out the wire, another straights it, a third cuts it, a fourth points it, a fifth grinds it at the top for receiving the head; to make the head requires two or three distinct operations; to put it on, is a peculiar business, to whiten the pins is another; it is even a trade by itself to put them into the paper; and the important business of making a pin is, in this manner, divided into about eighteen distinct operations, which, in some manufactories, are all performed by distinct hands, though in others the same man will sometimes perform two or three of them. I have seen a small manufactory of this kind where ten men only were employed, and where some of them consequently performed two or three distinct operations. But though they were very poor, and therefore but indifferently accommodated with the necessary machinery, they could, when they exerted themselves, make among them about twelve pounds of pins in a day. There are in a pound upwards of four thousand pins of a middling size. Those ten persons, therefore, could make among them upwards of forty-eight thousand pins in a day. Each person, therefore, making a tenth part of forty-eight thousand pins, might be considered as making four thousand eight hundred pins in a day. But if they had all wrought separately and independently, and without any of them having been educated to this peculiar business, they certainly could not each of them have made twenty, perhaps not one pin in a day; that is, certainly, not the two hundred and fortieth, perhaps not the four thousand eight hundredth part of what they are at present capable of performing, in consequence of a proper division and combination of their different operations."*

Capitalism Misinterpreted

Smith regarded the division of labor as the source of wealth of a nation, and he tried to understand the economy of his time in terms of this idea. Since then, the division of labor has become one of the prisms through which economy and society have been interpreted. The idea that this single new element was primarily responsible for the creation of a totally new and different socioeconomic system has been taken for granted. In our minds, this unquestioning belief in the division of labor and its effects is a mistaken one.

Let us now begin to use a different prism in interpreting the Industrial Revolution and the division of labor. We have stated that humanity's desire to be independent of nature manifested itself through work, part of which was the creation of economy, the transformation of natural forces into productive ones. As part of this economy, labor can also be interpreted as a transformation process: Manual labor would be seen as the transformation of our natural physical forces into productive forces, contingent upon our ability to control these forces mentally and use them in a purposeful activity.

---

* Smith, Adam. *The Wealth of Nations.* Chicago: A Phoenix Book, University of Chicago Press, 1976, pp. 7–9.

Given the development of this ability and its successful application, we find that, for a whole epoch in the history of humankind the production process was based primarily on the firsthand experience of the laborers, and that it continued at about the same level as this experience was transferred, relatively unchanged, from one generation to the next. The knowledge and experience necessary for a given trade was gained in the trade itself and passed directly from parent to child or from master craftsman to apprentice. There was little room for the introduction of changes that might have raised the production process to a higher level of efficiency.

The Contribution of the Organizer

The essence of the Industrial Revolution is actually found in a revolutionary improvement in production methods. While perhaps the most obvious characteristic of this new economy was the division of labor, the revolutionary new element in it was the fact that production was no longer based solely on the firsthand experience of the laborers. A new actor had arrived on the economic scene—the organizer, who introduced new ideas and methods to the production process and so improved the effectiveness of labor; through the organizer, the entire production process was raised to a higher intellectual level. *Thus, the Industrial Revolution can be regarded primarily as a revolution in the level of the thinking on which production was based.*

The division of labor was certainly one of the outstanding products of the application of thought to labor, but it was not the only revolutionary element. The division of labor—breaking the labor process up into a number of simple operations—made the use of new tools possible. Complex machinery was developed and used to perform operations that had previously been done with simple hand tools. The division of labor increased the opportunity for the thinking person to apply genius and creativity to the production process: Not only were new methods and machines created and used but, once the machines were invented, it became desirable to develop new forms of energy to run them. Watermills were an effective means of putting natural forces to work but their use was restricted to areas where rivers existed. The search for a new source of energy, a *new transformer,* to replace human labor soon produced a revolutionary invention—the steam engine.

Thus, the application of a higher level of thinking to the economy is the essence of the Industrial Revolution, and from it sprang more opportunities for further thought to be applied. As drops of water combine to make a stream, and streams join to make a river, so the endless stream of thoughts that followed the division of labor created the rush of progress called the Industrial Revolution.

The Age of Invention

About 1760, a wave of inventions started to change England. In the iron industry, charcoal began to be replaced by coke in converting pig iron into bar iron. Henry Cot, a navy agent, took out patents for puddling and rolling. James Hargreaves, a weaver and carpenter, devised a hand machine called the "Jenny," by means of which a worker could spin six or seven, and, later, eighty, threads at once. Richard Arkwright, a barber and wigmaker, with the help of John Kay, a clockmaker, used rollers to draw out the rovings before these passed to the spindle, and started the first revolution in the textile industry. Water-driven textile factories were also set up. Samuel Crompton, a weaver, produced a yarn suitable for both warp and weft, and adapted it to the production of all kinds of textiles.

Francis Home, a professor, showed how sulphuric acid could be used for bleaching in place of sour milk. John Roebuck made use of vitriol and salt to produce soda for soapmakers, white lead for potters, and litharge for glassworks.

The geologist James Hutton extracted sal ammoniac from soot, and coal began to be exploited as a source of chemicals—in the beginning, mainly for the production of tar and pitch necessary for the shipping industry. Josiah Wedgwood was instrumental in building a pottery industry. The engineering industry began to develop, and a canal from the coal mines at Worsley to Manchester and aqueducts were erected. A canal-and-road system was built, and bridges were also constructed. The production of engines became an industry of its own.

Before 1760, the number of patents granted in a single year hardly exceeded 12. In 1766, it rose to 31; in 1769, to 36; in 1783, to 64; in 1792, to 85; and in 1825 to 250.

James Watt and the Revolutionary Transformer

Yet by far the most important invention was that of James Watt, who invented a new mode of transforming natural forces into productive forces and began a process in which the typical force of production became a natural one, lying outside the human body. In sum, Watt replaced human work with engines.

At the University of Glasgow, Joseph Black was delivering lectures on latent heat, his own scientific discovery. Concurrently, John Anderson, who was in Black's class in natural philosophy, made a model of the steam engine, and Watt, a mathematical-instrument maker, was entrusted with its repair.

Watt had many consultations with Black and Anderson, and invented a separate condenser that could be kept cool while the cylinder remained hot. He also made plans for a full-scale engine, although it took some years before he built this revolutionary device.

The importance of Watt's invention lies in the fact that he was among the first to apply the methods of systematic experiment used in pure science—*scientific thinking*—to industry. He also synthesized the ideas and skills of others in order to create a complex mechanism. And so a revolutionary element, that of *integration,* was invented and applied to production, and a new era began.

From Division to Integration

The division of labor meant the division of what a single worker produced into separate and discrete operations. In the case of Watt, we find an integration of different types of work: scientific, mental, and manual. This integration of working effort, which does not eliminate the division of labor but creates a new and higher stage of development, became a general trend—one that was soon typical of a mature economy. As an example, an assembly line in a car factory is a common instance of the division of labor, yet the production of the car itself integrates practically all branches of industry, including the educational system, research enterprises, and banking.

This brings us back to our concept of the organizers and their essential role. The point that must be emphasized is that the division of labor did not in itself create the new economic system; its revolutionary impact was dependent upon the presence of the new element we have termed the organizer. Organization made it possible to apply a new and higher level of thinking to a process that had formerly been tied to the firsthand experience and skill of the workers, and so raised that process to a higher level.

The essence of the Industrial Revolution is to be found in the new production methods made possible by human intellectual ability—methods that replaced the work of humans with natural forces controlled by humans—and in the development of these revolutionary methods to the point that in many instances manual labor was rendered obsolete.

Where Marx and Others Failed

Although the classical theorists, and particularly Marx, observed and wrote about the role of human intellectual ability in economic development, the concept that productive processes and their management are based on the level of this ability did not enter into their theories, and was not considered an important element in the economy. But the founders of economics, whatever their theoretical school of thought, should not be criticized too harshly for this omission. In their time, these phenomena were just beginning to exert an influence, and the most typical productive force was still manual labor. Yet in today's mature economies, where the application of ability to think has become typical, neither the role of this intellectual level nor that of mental work is projected into economics either by the pupils of the classics of capitalism or by those of socialism.

Development in Agriculture and Business

Thus far, we have attempted to describe the revolution in thinking in the latter half of the 18th century as it applied to industry. A new intellectual level was also developed and applied to the production of agricultural goods at this time, though the situation was far less dramatic. Several new crops —the turnip, the potato—were introduced, and simple fertilizers such as marl and clay were added to sandy soil to enrich it. Crops began to be rotated; fens and marshes were drained; old, rough, and common pastures, were cultivated; and land was hedged to make it more productive for both crops and livestock. The substitution of wheat for inferior cereals, increased consumption of vegetables, the invention of soap, the use of brick instead of timber, and many other similar developments led to a remarkable improvement in the standard of living, and to a lowering of the death rate and an increase in population.

The management of business enterprises also moved to a new intellectual level—a move that was characterized by the emergence of the entrepreneur. Entrepreneurs were the organizers, the coordinators, and the businesspeople for given enterprises. They tried to buy and produce as cheaply as possible and to sell for maximum profit. They were concerned with inventions and innovations to make their own enterprises more profitable. They had to allocate resources, apply new technology, create markets for new products, and eliminate those for old ones. They also had to increase efficiency, acquire new capital, and think in terms of what was best for their businesses in the long run.

A Lack of Human Concern

We have described the Industrial Revolution from a perspective essentially different from the traditional one. Clearly, this period was a classic example of the human's attempt to become less dependent upon nature and thus a more independent being. This freedom was the result of thinking human beings creating conditions under which manual labor was reduced and replaced by the transformation of natural forces into productive ones and, consequently, achieving greater output.

The by-products of this new economy were many, and we have already noted some of the inventions, the new modes of production, the advances in transportation and agriculture, all of which helped to improve people's lives. Less obvious, however, are the negative elements that grew out of this new economic system. Indeed, the tremendous changes in the Industrial Revolution were accompanied by an amazing growth of wealth on the one hand and a process of impoverishment on the other. This was the point at which the new economy emerging from this revolution went astray.

People became fascinated by the wealth-creating potential of capital. Money, machinery, land, natural resources, and even human beings came to be regarded only in terms of their ability to contribute to the creation of wealth. Everything was viewed either as capital or as a means of acquiring capital. Some succumbed to their drive to produce more capital and, therefore, saw nothing except capital as remuneration for their effort. Others withdrew to make life as easy as possible for themselves, and did not participate in the evolutionary drive that took place at that time.

The idea that the people themselves, as the creators of this system, were responsible for its orientation and that the people themselves could be the visible hands and heads that turned the economy toward more humane goals was not considered. Instead, they were told that they should do nothing and leave everything to the invisible hand.

A major critic of this fascination with capital and its impact on society was Karl Marx. Unconscious of the liberating force of the human mind, he, too, considered the Industrial Revolution to be primarily a revolution in production rather than a revolution in thinking. Because of this focus on the wealth-creating potential of the system instead of on its ability to increase people's freedom through the application of thinking, Marx and other social critics directed their fire at the form of ownership, and identified the social system by the form of ownership. This interpretation of our economies has been the central issue of social and international conflicts, and even of wars: wars against nations, wars against our natural environment, and wars against ourselves and the human spirit in us.

The effect of this misinterpretation has been so far-reaching as to influence almost everyone's perception of world politics and economics. We have become accustomed to think in terms of capital and capitalism on one side and socialism and communism* on the other. It will be necessary to clarify these concepts and the conflict they have created before turning to the next revolution in our economic development.

* Marx conceived of socialism as the first stage in the development of a society with no private ownership. In this system, everyone would work according to his ability and be rewarded according to his effort. The last stage of this development, communism, describes a system in which everyone works according to his ability and is rewarded according to his needs. In America, the distinction between socialism and communism is very different: Socialism refers to systems incorporating social welfare, such as socialized medicine, although private ownership is not abolished, while communism refers to a system in which private ownership *and* democracy have been eliminated.

4

The
Scientific–
Technological
Revolution

From the Division to the Integration of Labor

The best way of becoming aware of the effects of the Scientific-Technological Revolution on production and the economy is to examine the making of a commodity that was produced both before and after this revolution took place. If we take shoes as our example, we can contrast the current modes of production with those of the industrial and preindustrial periods as well.

Before the Industrial Revolution, the production of shoes began with the farmer who raised the cattle for leather and grew the grain to feed them. Processing the hides was the tanner's work; he had to buy them from the farmer either for money or, more commonly, in exchange for goods such as finished leather. Once the hides had been tanned, the shoemaker's work began. He was responsible for the cutting and stitching of the leather and the completion of the final product. Through the cooperation of these three autonomous economic units—the farmer, the tanner, and the shoemaker—perhaps two pairs of shoes a week found their way into the hands of the people who had ordered them. But in a fairly primitive economy even this type of cooperation was infrequent, simply because the demand for shoes was low; production for individuals rather than for the market was the norm.

With the Industrial Revolution came the division of labor and consequent advances in production. The farmer now had the advantages of an increased knowledge of agricultural technique and perhaps a few hired hands to help with the running of the farm, and his production of grain and cattle increased. The tanner had also gained knowledge and experience. Perhaps he now ran a small factory staffed with five or six people and also used new chemicals or techniques, or even machines, to help him turn out finished leather of better quality and in greater quantity. It was the same for the shoemaker. He certainly employed people to help him in his trade and, eventually, to run the newly invented machines, which saved time and increased his output; he may have opened a shoe "store" to make more types of footwear available to the public. Now money rather than goods was changing hands, and production for the market was rapidly increasing. Thus, the cooperation of the farmer, the tanner, and the shoemaker became very important in the production process.

At today's level of economic development, the production of shoes is no longer quite so simple. The Scientific-Technological Revolution has created an integrated system involving far more components than just the farmer, the tanner, and the shoemaker, or even the separate industries they have become. Cooperation between these separate, autonomous units is a description used only by the superficial observer; the economic reality is completely different.

Beginning with the growing of grain and the raising of cattle, we find that the farmer is only one of a number of individuals involved. Farmers now specialize only in the growing of grain, and this in itself involves an army of workers, scientists, researchers, and administrators who produce the chemical fertilizers, tractors, trucks, and other equipment, develop the specialized grains and methods of planting, growing, and harvesting, and devise all the other agricultural techniques that have become industries in themselves. Equally complex is the cattle-raising industry, which now specializes in supplying the population with meat as well as with leather. The same is true for the processing of the hides; the tanning industry now makes use of highly sophisticated chemical treatments and machines and carries out research in the development of synthetic leather. In the shoe factories of the multitude of shoe manufacturers, we may observe a complete division of labor on assembly lines, as well as machines, offices for bookkeeping, administration, research, distribution, and marketing, all of which have become essential to keeping shoe stores all over the world stocked with the thousands of different types and styles of shoes and boots now offered to the public. All of this is, of course, supported by a huge communications and transportation system, a banking system, an educational system, and even governmental administration. Clearly, the application of science and technology to the production process has effected revolutionary changes in economy and in the society that supports it.

Three Stages of Economic Development

Here we have a somewhat simplified description of the integrated economic system that was created by the Scientific-Technological Revolution. While cooperation does exist between the separate components of this system, it is a limited cooperation compared with that of past economies. Far more typical for an economy at this stage of development is the integration of separate, autonomous, and frequently unrelated economic units into the production process. The existence of this integration process is clearer when we realize that a pair of shoes could not have been produced in today's economy without the educational system, or the banking system, or any of the other systems we have mentioned. Yet at the same time there is no direct cooperation between them. We could take any commodity produced today and find that many different activities or systems are essential to its production, but we could not state the exact share of these activities in the production process.

The integration process can be broken down historically into three separate levels, or stages, that span the past few hundred years. Before the Industrial Revolution, cooperation and production for the market were occasional—necessary whenever there was a demand for goods that could not be produced by an individual. The Industrial Revolution was based on the division of labor and cooperation between autonomous economic units, and production became geared toward the market. Currently, we have an economy in which the division of labor exists, but the integration of separate components into the production of single commodities has become typical. Production is no longer geared toward small, local markets but toward the nation and the world. The process of integration has expanded the economic realm and is about to create a world economy made up of one gigantic integrated system.

The Organically Integrated System

The mature economy resembles an organic system, and, as in an organic system, the separate components can be interpreted only in terms of the whole. We are aware, for instance, that the human body contains different organs—a brain, a heart, blood, eyes, kidneys, and lungs—all essential to the body's proper functioning, each having a specific role. Yet we are also aware, of course, that our eyes do not see by themselves; *we* see through the organs that we call eyes. Similarly, blood circulates in our bodies, but this is a completely different type of circulation from the mechanistic one of water circulating through pipes, and blood circulation is dependent upon the system of which it is a part. Further, water entering our system changes its properties and becomes part of the organism; a drop of blood chemically analyzed and defined outside the body is not really understood—its properties and functions can be understood only in terms of the system in which it is used. This type of thinking—organic rather than mechanistic—is what we should begin to use in studying the economy and its separate components and their functions. In this way, we shall come to stop thinking of the economy in terms of a mechanical, or "bookkeeping," approach.

The Whole Is More Than the Sum of Its Parts

Another part of our new understanding of economy must be the awareness that elements which make up the integrated socioeconomic system and its components, the "cells" of the organism, are in fact thinking human beings. From this will come the realization that the development of the economy is the result of our own development in thinking and our ability to create. In addition, it is important to realize that the system as a whole has properties which are different from and greater than the sum total of the properties of its separate components. We can again use the analogy of the human body to help clarify this point.

Now, the human organism contains many different components or subsystems. Each of them has a special role and function, and they are all essential to the proper functioning of the human body. Still, the human body as a whole has properties and functions that are different from those of its components. Further, although the body's subsystems have different functions, an interdependence exists between them, and between them and the body as a whole, and without the cooperation of all the separate subsystems the body will operate inefficiently or not at all. As an example, all the organs of the body may be perfectly healthy, but a blood disease, or a disease involving the cells that make up our organs and the body as a whole, such as cancer, will cause gradual deterioration of bodily functions and eventually will result in death.

We all know a forest is much more than the properties of the individual trees that make it up, and this same method of thinking can be applied to economics. (In fact, the idea of not being able to see the forest for the trees could be easily applied to most of today's economic theorists.) Towns are more than their buildings and populations, schools are more than their students and teachers, families are more than their individual members; these ideas are not new to us. In the economy, similar principles apply.

Our factories and banks, our transportation and communications systems may all operate perfectly well, yet "bad blood," such as problems with the money supply, will cause inflation and unemployment, and suddenly our capital, technology, and other abilities are of no use to us; the economy will break down in spite of them. The same "perfect economy" will cease to function properly if the "cells," the people who created it, lose their commitment to work, their sense of responsibility, or their expectations, or if they begin to distrust the government or disagree with the distribution of wealth. Our economy could not function properly with an inefficient banking or educational system, even though all the other components were operating at peak efficiency. Finally, the economy may flourish if its direction meets the expectations of the individuals involved, or, in the same way, it may break down if this is the product of ruthless egotism and selfishness. Herein lies the necessity of understanding the importance of the humanistic values of the Judeo-Christian philosophy and their incorporation into the socioeconomic system.

Commodity Barter and the Birth of Money

At a very low level of economic development, occasional barter took place. A surplus of certain goods for one individual or group and a shortage of the same goods for others brought people together, and exchanges of goods of equal value were made. As the economy developed and barter became more frequent, it was necessary to find something that would facilitate this type of trade. It became more difficult to find someone with a surplus and needs that would match the needs and surplus of someone else, and a commodity was needed that could be generally accepted as a means of exchange. At different times and in different places, shells, leather, tobacco, and metals were barter commodities. In an economy of this type, it was desirable, but not inevitable, to trade with this barter commodity. The economy could function without it, and so its role was that of simplifying, but not replacing, the bartering process.

These barter commodities were the first and most primitive form of "money." This "commodity money" functioned as a means of exchange and, as such, a measure of value, and was the typical form of money in its first stage of development. Any object having this property of "commodity money" does so partly because the object itself has value and partly because those who use it accept it as a means of exchange.

Money as a Product of the Economy

More important, however, is the idea that the kind of economy we are discussing had properties that made this form of barter, "commodity barter," and the use of "commodity money" reasonable and therefore possible. This type of economy was based on a rather low level of thinking as far as production and exchange were concerned; "commodity money" was a product of this level of thinking. The point is that we cannot understand "commodity money" or any other form of money simply on the basis of the properties or functions of the commodity; we must also see it in terms of the respective economy or society of which it is a part. Unless a society accepts a certain commodity as a means of exchange and a measure of value, that commodity cannot function as money.

As economic development continued, larger and more complex communities were created, and trade within and between communities grew. This development became possible because the whole of economic life shifted to a higher level of thinking. People involved in the production process gained experience, their labor became more productive, and new products and methods of production were discovered.

58

The "Commodity Money" Stage

In time, commodities such as silver, and particularly gold, came to be accepted as the general equivalents for all values. They made the exchange of goods and services easy and reliable, they were accepted as a means of payment throughout the world, and their units of weight were accepted as units of price. Because of this, they have been accepted as money for many centuries. In fact, we find that as far back as the seventh century B.C., "coins," or roughly stamped pieces of metal made of a mixture of silver and gold, were used either by the Lydians or the Ionians. The Chinese were also makers of coins, and introduced paper money as well.

Thus, during the first stage in the development of money, that of "commodity money," we find that as the economy developed and the exchange of goods expanded from that within a single community to that between communities, and then between countries, so the commodities used as "commodity money" changed as well. Grain and other goods were gradually replaced by silver and gold, which were more widely accepted, and the efficiency of economic performance was consequently increased. In this process, because trading became easier, the function of "commodity money" went from being a *means of exchange* and a *measure of value* to being a *means of payment,* a *unit of price,* a substance of inherent value. (In contemporary economics textbooks, we are told that money is defined in terms of these three functions or properties. According to this definition, they are characteristic of money in all economies, those of antiquity as well as of the present.)

Gold and gold coins have always had a great advantage in that the purchasing power of gold and of silver has always been relatively stable. They also had great disadvantages, however, and these became apparent as trade between communities and nations became more intensive. There was the danger of theft, the costs and risk of transportation, the loss of weight through abrasion, clipping and chipping, and the absence of interest or any other return for money. Because of this, wealthy merchants or goldsmiths became custodians and gave IOUs that could be used for further payment, instead of having the gold and silver transported. Further development led to the establishment of the first "banks" and a "deposit credit" evidenced by a "book entry."

As time passed, the developing economy needed more money; business enterprises were producing more goods, and trade was becoming more frequent than ever before. The production of gold and silver, however, did not always keep pace with the increase in the demand for money, and a new mode of production of money began to develop. The "bankers" found that they had to hold only a fraction of the total amount of gold and silver over which they had custody, because all the "depositors" did not withdraw their deposits at the same time. Rather than let this money sit idle, they began to lend some of it, and thus created an increase in the means of payment—in the money supply. These banking practices led to the replacement of "commodity money" with the "promise to pay."

"Commodity-Backed Money" and "the Promise to Pay"

With the development of the primitive banking system, the actual gold and silver were gradually replaced by the "promise-to-pay" gold and silver, typically in the form of a written IOU, or, less frequently, simply by a verbal promise. Goods are not being exchanged, nor is the "commodity money" of gold changing hands, at least initially. The document (or word) has no value in itself; its value lies in the fact that it is backed by a valuable commodity (gold or silver), and, of course, that it is accepted by those involved.

A further stage in the development of money was characterized by a gradual increase in the use of this promise to pay in the economy. Beginning with the bankers and other wealthy businessmen who used it to make loans and in transactions involving large sums, *"commodity-backed money"* soon came to be the only form of money, completely replacing that of "commodity money," which was far less efficient at the new and higher level of economic development that existed. (The silver certificates that were used until recently in the United States were typical of this "commodity-backed money," and, in fact, stated that the federal government "will pay to the bearer on demand One Dollar" in sterling silver.) The use of the promise to pay not only increased the efficiency of economic performance but also had a tremendous and permanent effect on the relationship of money to the economy.

The Unnoticed Revolution

The emergence of "commodity-backed promise to pay" was actually a great revolution in monetary history, and one that, unfortunately, was not perceived as such by our economic theoreticians. While they did make the distinction between "commodity money" and "commodity-backed money," they failed to see the revolutionary impact caused by the emergence of "the promise to pay" as the typical means of payment in connection with the emergence of the new economic system after the Industrial Revolution. As a consequence, these changes were not included in the theories of our economists.

The Organic System

It will further our understanding of this radical change in the function of money and its revolutionary impact if we return briefly to our concept of an organic system and how it differs from a mechanical one. We know that when water circulates in a system of pipes, a mechanical system, it continues to be water and does not change. When water enters an organic system such as a plant or the human body, however, its properties change. While it is natural for us to speak of the "water" in our bodies as blood or urine, we do not make a parallel distinction with money; because of our conventional mechanistic approach to the economy, we perceive money simply as "water in a system of pipes." By failing to realize that the postindustrial economic system is similar to an organic one, we are not aware that the concept of money has basically changed as well.

"Money" Changes as the Economy Changes

Let us now consider the origin of the new monetary function.

We have already pointed out that, as part of the economic process, the properties of "money" change according to the system of which that money is a part. Consequently, "money" does not exist in itself; it exists only as a component of an economic system. If, for example, we destroyed our contemporary economy and the society that supports it and returned to the primitive society of cavemen, our "money," our precious bills and coins, would cease to be of any use or value. Thus, changing the economic system results in a change in the properties of "money."

This is the basic answer to the question of how "money" changed. At the risk of repetition, we can gain a better understanding of the way in which "money" changed and the reasons for it by looking again at the economy at the time of the Industrial Revolution and some decades after it.

The Economy of Barter and Cooperation

At the beginning of the Industrial Revolution, the economy was composed chiefly of autonomous units, and its functioning was based primarily on cooperation. The farmer was one autonomous unit. Methods of production were relatively simple, and whatever products were needed to operate the farm—a cart or some tools—could either be built by the farmer or bought from a neighboring wheelwright or blacksmith in exchange for agricultural goods. The sale of these goods on the market, through a merchant, was infrequent, for the goods the farmer produced were widely accepted as a means of exchange, and it was more convenient for the farmer to deal directly with the producers of the materials needed. Similarly, the blacksmith, the tanner, and other craftsmen, producers in their own right, could exchange their goods for those of a specific producer, although, because the need for their products was not as great as the need for the farmer's goods, they were more apt to sell whatever surplus goods they produced on the market instead of through barter.

In general, then, each of these independent economic actors was a producer of some kind of consumer good that could be exchanged with other producers for the goods they needed; this was, in fact, the essence of their autonomy. Further, the degree of cooperation with regard to this exchange of goods and their respective value was such that the barter system remained a viable form of economic activity. Clearly, in such an economic system, cooperation among these separate producers was essential for their survival and for the proper functioning of the system.

As the Industrial Revolution developed and factories emerged, a growing portion of manufactured goods was produced specifically for the market rather than simply for exchange. This shift was due to the fact that production no longer involved only the manufacture of consumer goods. Machinery and other materials used in the new methods of production that had been developed were now increasingly in demand. At this stage in the economy, the production of raw material and semiraw material for further production—

steel, iron, and the parts necessary for the manufacture of new machines and engines—had become an industry in itself, and its products were traded on a special market. A perfectly new type of economic activity, the production of materials and tools used in production, had evolved.

Barter Becomes Outmoded and Money Changes

Step by step, the economy ceased to be a system of barter. It was no longer possible for a shoe factory to pay for what it needed from the machine-tool industry with the goods it had produced, or for the machine-tool industry to give a foundry its machines in exchange for steel. Similarly, those who worked in these factories could not be paid for their time and energy with the actual products of their labor.

In this new economy, the properties of "money" changed. The "commodity money" of goods that supported the barter system was no longer practical or reasonable, because the economy that was developing through the Industrial Revolution had made barter impossible. "Money" no longer existed simply as a means of exchange between producer and consumer. It was forced by the economy to become *a means of payment* between the producers themselves. As time went on, the "promise to pay" came to dominate the economic system.

The economy of the early stages of the Industrial Revolution could be described as a mechanistic system. While craftsmen expanded their businesses into small factories, they maintained their autonomy as producers, and production was still the result of cooperation, although between factories rather than simply between individuals. Yet in the development of the production process from that based on autonomous individuals to one of autonomous factories, the nature of this cooperation changed and brought with it a change in the character of "money."

5

Money and Its Real Function

The Revolutionary Quality: Money as a Catalyst

The new economic system that was born in the Industrial Revolution and matured during the Scientific-Technological Revolution is, as noted, an "organic" system. And it is because of this "organic" system that a new function of "money" emerged in the second stage of its development.

New Means of Payment

This stage has been closely connected with the rapid economic development produced by the Scientific-Technological Revolution. In it, we can observe the emergence of a different type of means of payment, and, although many of us have experienced the change, it is one we may be only dimly aware of. The speed of economic development caused by the Scientific-Technological Revolution has created the need for more "money" than there is gold to back it. So we made a new form of money: paper money. We accept mere paper money simply because it is a part of the economy. There is no other way to run such a highly developed economy but by using mere paper. It is backed not by commodities but by economic performance. If the economy does not perform, the money loses its purchasing power.

The Domination of Credit

The changes that characterize the latest stage in the development of "money" become more and more dominant in our economic system as time passes.

We have reached a stage in the development of both the economy and of "money" when credit has become the typical means of payment. We can conceive of the economy functioning without the coins and bills issued by the government but not without a banking and credit system and the billions of book entries from which these systems have developed. Certainly, we have entered the stage at which "credit" has become the precondition for our economy's smooth and efficient functioning.

Just compare a few figures from the American economy that are typical for any highly developed economy. There is about $89 billion in circulation. This currency is legal tender, issued by the government, and is *actual* money. Consumer credit amounts to nearly $200 billion, corporate bonds amount to $315 billion, the public debt amounts to more than $600 billion; the total of all credits in the economy amount to three trillion dollars. Legal-tender money is negligible compared to the amount of credits and the twenty billion bookkeeping entries through which these credits are passed back and forth and on which the economy is actually based.

In short, we have a new economic "body," but our economists stick to old definitions or definitional statements, not at all derived from our economic reality. The *actual* money supply is relatively stable, depending solely on the government. Nobody but the government or its agencies may issue legal-tender money. Yet the economy depends to a decisive extent on the credit supply. Credit supply changes every second, each book entry actually representing such a change. Economists also speak of the circulation of money in the same way as people spoke of circulation of gold coins in the past. Actually, the circulation of money is negligible; what is decisive is the intensity of book entries, but this is disregarded in the calculations of too many economists, since it does not fit neatly into conventional monetary theory.

Apart from consumer credit, including credit cards, the bulk of credit is given to business enterprises and communities.

If the banks lend only for productive purposes, no harm, no inflation, no recession need occur. But if the banks lend money for unproductive purposes, much harm is done to the economy. If, for instance, money is lent to communities to meet the consequences of their mismanagement, such loans have an inflationary impact. The same applies, of course, to the government. Any layperson will appreciate that it is not the amount of credit available that matters but for what purpose it is being used. Not the quantity but the quality matters. Of course, the layperson seldom has to distinguish between money and credit. People get a salary in checks—actually a book entry—and may pay all expenses with checks or credit cards (again book entries). It makes little difference whether one speaks of having money or having credit.

Yet on the level of the economy as a whole, there is a great difference. We have a new economy based on highly sophisticated production, and such an economy has developed not only specific commodities and services and new professions but also specific means of payment that could not have existed in a less developed economic "body" and without which our own economic "body" could not function. Let us now, approach the problem of monetary policy from this angle.

Monetary Policy

We shall begin by assuming that, as a general rule, everything that *can* be accomplished reasonably well by business enterprises, whether individually or collectively, *should* be accomplished by them without interference from the government. Only what is beyond the scope and capacity of business enterprises should and must be the concern of a central organ such as the government. The money supply and its purchasing power is one area that cannot be controlled by the thousands of banks, millions of savers, tens of thousands of business enterprises, or a similar number of agencies; this creates monetary chaos. Thus, according to conventional monetary theories, the government should be entrusted with complete control of the money supply to insure that the economy has as much money as is necessary for it to actualize its full potential for growth and productivity.

The question immediately arises as to where the government shall get all this "money." As we have seen, the concept of a money supply is really more of a fiction than a fact of economic reality; the real issue is one of giving credit of a scope that meets the needs of an economy functioning with full employment. This could be accomplished through the central bank of any nation, controlled by Congress or Parliament, which would be responsible for the issue and control of credit—the IOUs we need. Sufficient credit will never cause inflation so long as it is used for increased production. The present inflation occurred despite a tight "money supply." Without an adequate increase in production, wages, salaries and taxes increased, and inflation was the result.

The Establishment of a Credit Supply

Let us imagine that our credit system was put into effect. The central bank would be required to issue credit to independent commercial banks, but would not charge interest. Since the commercial banks wouldn't have to pay interest, the costs of bank credit to the commercial bank's customers would be reduced by approximately 50 percent. Since savings banks would not depend on savings deposits, and would not pay interest on them, mortgages and other loans would be offered at only 3 to 4 percent interest. (We should remember that the interest paid on savings accounts is only technically paid by the banks themselves. Actually, the cost of this interest is passed on by the banks to the consumer in the cost of loans and mortgages.) In almost every area involving interest rates and related costs, we could expect that the consumer would be charged that much less than at present, because those rates would be eliminated. The banks would have to charge only enough to cover their operating costs, and that of risk and profit.

The absence of interest paid on savings accounts under the credit system would not necessarily deter people from making deposits in these accounts. There would probably be a greater tendency to spend money, and people would invest in real estate, art, and other valuables, or in the stock market. However, "saving for a rainy day" would certainly not be eliminated, and the credit saved in banks could be used in much the same way as it is now. By lending these assets to customers or investing them, commercial banks could use their savings deposits to supplement the amount of credit issued by the central bank or to lower the amount of this credit. In either case, the economy would have the credit supply necessary for its efficient functioning, regardless of a specific household's tendency to save.

In addition, anyone who needed to borrow credit for certain business ventures, home improvements, or any other reason, would be able to do so under the conditions set up by individual banks. The central bank (or, for that matter, the government), while responsible for the credit supply, would not be involved in these credit contracts. The banks themselves would have the responsibility for setting up borrowing agreements, just as they do now.

The Advantages of a Credit System

At first glance, it might seem that the government and its banking agency would have a tremendous concentration of power under this new system. As a matter of fact, they would command far less power than they do now. The central bank would only have the *duty* of supplying credit to banks and making sure that they follow whatever regulations have been established. Its sphere of influence would be limited to these dealings with commercial banks, and under no circumstances would it be permitted to create credit relationships with individual business enterprises.

In contrast, the central banking system that exists today has a great deal of influence at the level of enterprise in its control over the money supply. In creating a shortage of money, and, consequently, unemployment, in controlling the interest rates and influencing the intentions to invest, and in its use of open-market operations—all of which central banks are empowered to do in order to regulate the money supply and prevent the economy from overheating—the central banks have a great effect on the performance of businesses.

In preventing the economy from overheating, central banks actually try to keep their national economies from operating at peak efficiency. Conventional economic theories teach us that an economy working at full capacity is danger-ous, in that it creates inflation. This, according to the theories, must be balanced out through unemployment. Consequently, full employment is seen as undesirable.

The Reduction of Inflation

Of course, we oppose inflation and have stated that we view it as a crime against man. While the importance of a stable price level will be discussed in a subsequent chapter, we must now ask whether offering an ample supply of credit to make the economy perform at full capacity would, in itself, create inflation.

Without deposits, commercial banks have no way of giving credit to business enterprises. Yet simply because they do have the ability to extend credit does not mean that they will haphazardly lend all their assets out. They will always be concerned with getting their equity and interest back, and will offer credit only where they can be assured of their return.

Under the current system, because banks pay interest for deposits, they are under pressure to lend in order to earn the interest they must pay to their depositors. Consequently, they take higher risks in lending to make money. Under our proposed new credit system, the credit supplied by the central bank is given free of charge. Thus, commercial banks will not be forced to take the risks they now take, and will be able to be far more concerned with the borrower's ability to repay. They will be more concerned that the credit will be used for efficient production, and so no inflation will occur.

Another point that should be borne in mind when discussing our credit system is the fact that the means of payment, or "money," is used in a different way in households than in business enterprises. In business, the general tendency is to spend assets only with regard to potential returns; if a business has more assets, it does not necessarily spend more —unless the expected returns justify this spending. Conversely, if a family's income increases, then that family will generally spend more, and so create inflationary pressure.

We believe that the theories of the conventional economists, which consider only the sum total of the money supply, overlook this important point. The question of the size of the money supply is not nearly so crucial as *where* it is: Is it in households, in banks, or in business? And if it is in business, for what purpose is it being used? For the production of consumer goods or of war machines? Is it in a well-run company or a mismanaged one? In the contemporary economy, the structure or distribution of the money supply is far more important than the total amount.

To talk about the total money supply, in fact, is as unhelpful as talking about the total rain supply of a country. What is important and useful to know is when, where, and at what time the rain falls. If all the rain falls during the harvest, it could ruin the harvest. If it falls at the proper time, it will increase the harvest.

In the economy as well, what mainly matters is for what purposes money and credit are used and to what extent it helps to make full use of unemployed labor, underutilized productive capacities, and so on.

New Responsibility for Banks

A further advantage to the new credit system is the fact that the banks and the economy as a whole would not be dependent on how much people deposit, as they are now. The central bank would be the main depositor in the commercial banks. And it would be the responsibility of the central bank to supply the economy with ample credit supply through its deposits in the commercial banks. These deposits would be at the disposal of the commercial banks, with the understanding that credit would be given on strictly sound business terms. Thus, as we have said, business efficiency would be fostered.

As a by-product, the system would prevent direct interference by the government at the level of individual business. Credit could not be misused for political ends. Commercial banks would have the new function of letting out the proper amount of credit for the maximal productivity of the economy.

This system could be compared to a great reservoir of water. A gardener will use water from the reservoir for flowers, but the amount of water taken is not governed by the size of the reservoir as long as there is plenty of water available and it isn't rationed. Instead, the amount taken is governed by what the individual flowers need. The reservoir symbolizes the credit supply of the central bank, and the gardener the commercial banks. These will draw from the credit reservoir only the credit that is needed by individual enterprises that the banks judge to be good risks.

The New Role of the Government

The establishment of a credit supply would give the national government greater responsibility for the functioning of the economy as a whole because of its duty to supply the economy with sufficient credit. And yet it would have less power to interfere with business by manipulating, as it does now, the money supply. Under the new system, the government would no longer be able to decrease the money supply or alter the interest rates. By reducing this type of government interference, we could reduce the scale of the bureaucracy as well. Thus, using the efficient banking that now exists, this new system would create a bridge between the macroeconomic policy of the government and the microeconomic sphere of business enterprises, and prevent direct interference by the government or the central banking system in the economy proper. The duties of the government would include the creation of the preconditions for full employment by offering sufficient credit for that purpose; it would not act specifically to create full employment in itself.

Consequently, we could throw overboard the harmful concept of *government spending,* in which the government is supposed to spend the taxpayers' money to employ the unemployed directly or indirectly. Instead, we introduce the concept of *government lending,* where the government offers to the banking system credits free of charge in order to supply the economy with as much credit as needed—with the proviso that the credit will be used for productive purposes and will be repaid.

From this angle, we could immediately turn to some practical steps. For example, we could introduce the concept of government lending to the construction industry. The Government would deposit non-interest-bearing treasury bills or other IOUs in the central bank, and the central bank would offer credits earmarked for housing to the banking system, with no interest charged. The banks would simply offer loans; and the rate of interest would, consequently, be lower than the present rate by something like 6 percent.

Such loans could be earmarked for low-income and

middle-income housing, and would take into consideration construction and insulation that save fuel. Even inexpensive solar units could be financed from these credits. Such credits might also be extended to repairs of low-income and middle-income housing and other areas. Thus, an environmental and fuel-conservation consideration could be applied. We could combine these credits with an anti-inflationary clause, meaning that a kind of price ceiling on the buildings would be attached to the credits.

Subsidies are costly and must be repaid by taxes—and so they burden the consumer and are inflationary. However, to offer a greater credit supply would immediately increase production and employ a number of unemployed and offer housing to those who need it but cannot afford it at the present cost of mortgages.

Parallel to such measures, we would recommend that not only on the level of states or provinces but also down to the level of towns and cities contingency plans for similar credit supplies should be worked out. The trade unions would find a new and constructive way to care for their unemployed members in working out contingency plans to make full use of unemployed labor in their towns or cities.

We are convinced not only that the economic situation would improve but also that we could fight the current doomsday prophecies, that we would orient our thinking toward positive and humane solutions, that we could demonstrate how the government can help the economy without new departments, institutions, and bureaucracy, and particularly without any interference in and limitations on free enterprise.

There are further practical conclusions to be derived from the understanding of the role of money and, particularly, how to avoid inflation even under conditions of full employment.

We are aware that the concept of government spending

as an aid to the economy has become a deep-rooted concept, accepted both by theoreticians and by laypeople influenced by the mass media; and now we find it useful to consider *government lending* versus *government spending* as one of the key issues of our economy.

6

Government Lending *vs.* Government Spending

The Birth of Government Spending

During the Great Depression, economists found that the economy could not, by itself, reduce the chaos created by extreme fluctuations in the rate of employment, and they came to realize the limitations of the economy's capacity for self-adjustment. The practical consequence of this was the development of theories justifying government spending. According to these theories, the government should be allowed to spend money in whatever amount and for whatever purpose necessary to raise the level of employment.

The newly employed would increase the demand for goods and services, and would, in turn, generate an increase in supply or production. In this way, government spending would lead to a more productive economy overall.

In the democratic world, the English economist John Maynard Keynes was one of the first to advocate government spending as a means of stimulating the economy, and his theories helped to pull the United States, as well as his own country, back from the brink of economic disaster. In Germany during the early thirties, some years before Keynes, Hitler's Minister of Economics, Hjalmar Schacht, eliminated unemployment by using government funds to create job opportunities in areas such as road construction, and particularly in areas relating to rearmament and other preparations for the coming war. Both of these Western economists were, however, preceded by Stalin and the methods of economic planning he introduced in the Soviet Union; government spending is actually one of the basic features of the Soviet economy, where the government's economic plan accounts for all the money the government intends to spend to insure the proper functioning of the entire socioeconomic system.

The political impact of the widespread unemployment that characterized the worldwide economic crisis of the thirties shook the democratic foundations on which Western civilization was based, and we must acknowledge the genius of Keynes and others like him and applaud their attempts to avert this crisis; the philosophy of government spending that they developed has, with minor changes, been accepted throughout the world. Unfortunately, this philosophy has become not only a justification for but also an invitation to inflation; it is, in part, responsible for the economic crisis of today. Because of this, our feeling is that the practice of government spending is one of the great tragedies in the development of conventional economics.

Tragic Consequences

Reckless government spending for other than productive purposes creates inflation and debts. Debts require the payment of interest, which in turn is charged to the people in the form of taxes. This practice and the philosophy that supports it undermines all economic rationality; it is demoralizing because it underestimates the value of true *productive* work; it is unfair because it burdens the consumer with higher taxes; and it is essentially harmful to the nation and the economy because the economy's potential for producing goods and services is used for no important or creative purpose.

Government spending makes the government take action in areas where it can only do more harm than good. It causes the government to become overinvolved in economic performance and, by creating new jobs and programs, to expand an already cumbersome and efficiency-inhibiting bureaucracy. By spending the nation's money without being concerned that it is spent for productive purposes, the government has to raise taxes that in turn are projected in prices, and so devaluates the very money it issues. This inflationary trend is then fought by increases in the rate of interest, decreases in the money supply, and even by the creation of unemployment.

The power of the central banking system of a nation

to fix the price of money through its control of interest rates, or that of the government to change both the rate of taxation and the quantity of the money supply, involves an extraordinary amount of interference with the workings of business enterprises. This interference inhibits production at the enterprise level and magnifies the economic crisis and its crippling effects on the nation.

Government spending focuses on isolated economic problems such as unemployment, and results in a continually expanding budget that must be met by a proportionate increase in taxes. Government spending for the sake of full employment is currently viewed as a function of the government, and the government budget of developed nations amounts to approximately a third of the gross national product of these countries.

Changing the Frame of Reference

The current economic crisis and the concept of government spending that supports it are largely the products of the way conventional economists view our economic system. As long as the economy is guided by outdated economic theories, as long as we think in terms of "money supply," the "budget," "government spending," and the government's responsibility to control and maintain an efficiently functioning economy, there is no other way to handle unemployment and low economic productivity except in the manner of Keynes, Schacht, or Stalin: through increased spending, expanding budgets, and higher taxes. By adhering to these theories and the monetary and fiscal policies they support, we shall perpetuate, rather than eliminate, our economic crisis, with all its tragic consequences.

From this, it follows that the beginning of the solution to our problems is to change our economic frame of reference. The concept of "credit supply," introduced in the previous chapter, is not only a realistic concept but also offers a completely different and effective approach to the problems we have described.

In an economy functioning with a "credit supply," the government agrees to give "credit" to the nation through commercial banks, and avoids direct interference with business enterprises and the economy. The crucial element in this concept is the idea that it is the government's *duty* to supply "credit," and in whatever amount necessary, for the efficient functioning of the economy. The government's responsibility ends at this point: economic efficiency in itself becomes the responsibility of the business enterprises. Again, the government's only responsibility is to provide enough money to make full employment and high productivity possible.

Lending vs. *Spending*

In this system, the practice of government spending is replaced by that of government lending. Let us begin our discussion of this new method of maintaining a high level of economic performance by contrasting it with the method currently being used.

Suppose that the government *spends* ten billion dollars for the building of roads or for some similar undertaking in order to fight unemployment. As we have mentioned, the money for this project is provided by taxes, and these are reflected in the prices of consumer goods and services. As a result, it is the consumer who pays. Higher prices, in turn, lead to wage increases and the continuation of the inflationary spiral. Since government spending must continue in order to maintain this high rate of employment, taxes will have to increase even further, and inflation will continue.

Through the concept of government *lending,* we approach the problem of unemployment and low economic productivity in a different way. Suppose, for instance, that unemployment exists in the housing industry. With an interest-free credit supplied by the government, commercial banks could offer a loan of perhaps ten billion dollars at a low rate of interest.

The essential difference here is that the government has *lent* the money rather than spent it. Theoretically, the loan would be repaid when the completed houses were sold; in practice, some new loans might be issued and some old loans might be repaid each day, and loans and repayments would roughly balance out. In either case, because money is supplied in the form of a loan, taxes and prices would not be affected; the ten billion dollars merely offers the opportunity for work and the construction of new homes. Furthermore, since the unemployment compensation paid by the government would be reduced and income and production would be increased, this loan might even raise the government's income, perhaps enabling it to lower the rate of taxation.

Earmarking Credits

This example suggests other important features of the concept of government lending. The first of these is the fact that a portion of the credit offered to commercial banks by the government could be earmarked for specific purposes or programs. The system of credit supply provides safeguards against the possibility that the credit lent would be used for unconstructive purposes. The earmarking of credit will insure that the more pressing problems of the economy and the nation—unemployment, for example—will be solved quickly. The main concern must not be the aggregate amount of credit supplied, but where and for what purpose it is used.

Developing Economic Democracy

Credits cannot be earmarked in a haphazard fashion; specifying their use is a difficult process that requires not only a vast amount of data but also a true understanding of the economy and the society. Programs that might qualify for earmarked credits must be carefully worked out so that credits will be used to deal effectively with real economic problems.

Because the programs will affect the entire nation, they must be concerned with human desires, needs, and expectations.

The new concern for economic functioning and the betterment of the quality of life of the nation will not necessarily be restricted to economic scientists. Not only could programs be developed by concerned students and teachers at various colleges and universities but organizations of committed citizens, consumer groups, and even business enterprises could set up research institutes to focus on specific economic or social problems. Trade unions might also interest themselves in such studies in order to give their members more protection and benefits. The alternative programs resulting from such a commitment and concern will certainly be many, and choices will have to be made, depending on the nation's priorities. The fact that so many people would be involved in formulating and selecting the programs would lead to a real economic democracy.

Alternative economic programs from a variety of sources must be chosen, and national and local economic priorities will have to be established. And since these programs and priorities will affect the whole nation, they should become issues in national elections. Furthermore, these programs will have to be implemented at state or province and local levels. The citizens of the communities involved must also be given the opportunity to express their views and to decide, democratically, how these programs will be carried out.

The Potential of Government Lending

The great potential of the system of government lending can be seen in its many and varied practical applications. For example, if unemployment exists in the automobile industry, or if automobile production is curtailed because of environmental consequences, government lending could be used to earmark credit for the development and production of more efficient systems of mass transportation, and the number of new jobs created by the loan would match, or even exceed, the number of people laid off. Credit might also be given to special industries so that unskilled workers could acquire knowledge and training.

Moving away from the business realm, government lending could be used to promote research by certain groups or organizations in areas of concern such as new sources of energy or methods of conservation. Households might receive credit earmarked for the installation of solar-energy units, and so this and other means of energy conservation would be promoted. Further, credit could be made available at the state or province or town level to promote the development of productive programs. In this context, we must again emphasize that these credits (given by the central bank to commercial banks) would be allocated on strictly commercial terms; they would not, as is the case with government spending, burden the taxpayer—the consumer. And because the credit will be used for *productive* purposes and will be repaid, inflationary pressure will not be created, and the government will have more freedom to offer loans directed toward the improvement of the socioeconomic system as a whole.

The Structure of the G.N.P.

In the past, economists have been concerned with making full use of a nation's labor supply in order to increase the gross national product. In fact, the practice of government spending grew out of this concern for a growing G.N.P. At this point in economic development, however, the size of the gross national product is no longer of primary importance. It is the *structure* of the G.N.P., and not its growth, that must become our main concern, and to this end we have proposed the concept of government lending.

While the concept of government spending is based on the principle of economic growth for its own sake, government lending requires that we turn our attention toward using our economic potential for constructive purposes. Rather than asking simply how to perpetuate the growth of the G.N.P., we must deal with more important and relevant questions. We must begin to ask, for example, whether we shall continue to pollute the environment and to waste, and so exhaust, our limited resources; whether we are concerned with social well-being or simply with economic growth; whether we are interested only in our own generation or can think of future generations as well; whether we can begin to have concern for the other, less fortunate inhabitants of the world.

Through a concern with the structure of the G.N.P. and the use of government lending, we can redirect our economic potential toward more humane ends. It is even possible that the G.N.P. might not grow. But by recycling, by using different raw materials and energies, by depolluting the environment, and by spending more money on education and culture, we could use our existing potential for the achievement of goals that benefit the nation as a whole. A new interest in the quality of life and our fellow humans, now and in the future, must take precedence over the current fascination with economic growth.

Any student of the Soviet type of economy knows that in the Soviet Union the gross national product shows a relatively rapid growth while the standard of living is hardly growing at all. The explanation is simple. The less that efficient investments are made and the more that material is used and wasted, the greater is the cost of what is produced. In other words, the higher the cost of the products, the higher the gross national product.

The theory of the gross national product is unfortunately applied also to the Canadian and American economies, and today we see a growing national product without adequate growth of the standard and quality of life. The concept of government spending is one of the most important components of this frightening development. We are taught that the growth of the gross national product is to be seen as a proof of a well-run economy, and that it should be regarded as an end in itself. Yet a growth of the G.N.P. can even be harmful if it produces less efficiently, or if we invest with no economic justification. Thus, we could invest more or spend more and have a greater G.N.P., but have produced fewer commodities and services. Through democratically controlled government lending, we could and should put greater emphasis on the structure of the G.N.P., and particularly on the extent to which it meets all needs—spiritual, cultural, and material —of the nation.

Meeting the Expectations of the Population

Although we have reached the point in economic development where most of the population is living far above the subsistence level, through the reorientation in economic thinking and practice we are discussing, the poverty that does still exist can be eliminated. Furthermore, there is much room for improvement in areas such as education, and for improvements that will produce a higher standard of living overall.

Yet the achievement of these goals will create new problems that will have to be solved. For example, a more educated nation will come to expect more from life in terms of quality and culture. This is first of all a human problem, but it has economic implications as well: if people are frustrated and unhappy with their socioeconomic system, the quality of their work suffers, and this, in turn, affects economic performance. The economic system must meet the needs and expectations of the population if it is to operate efficiently.

This fact has already had an impact at the enterprise level, where management science has begun to show a new concern for the welfare of employees. In his best-selling study, *Management,* Peter Drucker states that where management used to be responsible for helping employees adjust to the operation of the business, their approach has now changed to one of adjusting the operation of the enterprise to the needs of its employees. This principle must also be applied to the economic system as a whole.

The needs and expectations of the population are important factors in the economic efficiency of any nation, and should never be underestimated. Unfortunately, conventional economics has never taken this human element into account, and, consequently, its methods of controlling the economy have proved ineffective.

Reducing Government Interference

We must again state that the amount of credit to be earmarked would represent only a portion of the total amount of credit offered by the government. We would assume that this earmarked portion might be some 10 to 20 percent of the total, while the rest would be used for unspecific (though productive) purposes. Also, commercial banks would have their own assets, composed of the savings deposits of citizens and corporations.

The government's budgetary spending amounts to about a third of the nation's G.N.P., and this, coupled with its effects on taxes, gives the federal budget a tremendous impact on political, social, and economic life. In view of this, steps must be taken to insure that the government spends wisely.

One of the most logical ways of accomplishing this would be to submit the federal budget to the voters. In much the same way as the earmarked portions of the government credits supplied to the nation become objects of economic democracy, so the structure of the budget should become a topic of economic studies and an election issue as well. Economists would have to study a proposed budget carefully, determining the impact of the government's financial activities on the economy and the general quality of life of the citizens. Their report could be published and distributed nationally, and elections could be held to determine if the budget met with national approval.

Independent studies of the government's budget by economists and other groups not only would insure that the government's priorities were those of the people but could even help in debureaucratizing the entire government system. Such studies would certainly be concerned with the task of determining which programs and activities now funded by the government could be turned over to business enterprises and private organizations and funded through government lending. The budget could then be cut, taxes would be reduced, and those programs which have been crippled by bureaucratic red tape would be free to operate effectively.

We should take into consideration that in the United States and Canada—and, for that matter, in any highly developed economy—the sum total of taxes paid amounts to something like 50 percent of personal expenditures.

In a responsible society, the budget should express the principle of responsibility. This would mean that any programs proposed by the political parties should include the exact costs of these programs. An election would then not be attractive promises only, with no consideration of the costs the nation has to pay, but would become the expression of real concern for the interests of the nation. Each party could offer an estimate of the cost of its program for the whole election period, and the election competition would be based on comparing the potential costs and benefits of each program. Elections would then become a great economic school for the nation.

The concept of government spending makes such a practice impossible. The political parties may promise such things as full employment and social-welfare programs, but nobody knows how much they would cost. We have, therefore, a permanent growth of the budget and the national debt, and, consequently, of the interest to be paid on them. We would emphasize further that we are *not* critical of limited government spending, because the government has to spend for many important services it offers such as defense, maintenance of law and order, and public assistance. But we are critical of the *concept* of government spending that justifies any spending, even to finance employment for nonproductive purposes, as if employment were an end in itself.

If we introduce the concept of government lending, then full employment will be achieved by giving loans to the productive sector of the society, and so we will attain *both* full employment and a stable price level, for the increase in wages and salaries out of the credits will be matched by an increase of production.

Two Objections

We expect two major objections to our proposal of establishing a system of credit supply and introducing the practice of government lending. The first would be this: Simply offering credit to consumers and businesses does not guarantee that this credit will be used: unemployment and the economic system that causes it will not necessarily be affected by these proposals. This argument is supported by the fact that although credit is currently available for housing, those who need housing do not take out mortgages and do not build; many potential investments are not realized for reasons other than a lack of money or credit.

The second objection is that even if government lending does not produce the inflationary pressures created by government spending and higher taxes, wouldn't inflation be created by an economy functioning at peak capacity? This objection is based on the idea that economic booms and full employment inevitably lead to inflation, since both prices and wages have a tendency to rise. We will deal with this objection in the next chapter.

In answering the first objection, we would focus on an element generally neglected by conventional economic theory —that of the motivation behind one's decision to invest. To take just one example, under the current system a 10-year loan of $10,000 at 8.5 percent interest will mean that a borrower will have to repay $1,488 a year—nearly $15,000 over 10 years. In times of desperate uncertainty about one's future income, such a commitment represents too large a risk; enterprises as well as private individuals are simply afraid to invest.

Economy is more than the money supply, the rate of employment, the level of prices, and all the other terms with which conventional economists define the economic system. It is a system of thinking human beings—human beings with hopes, desires, fears, needs, and, with regard to investment, certain expectations. These expectations have a tremendous impact on one's economic actions.

At present, everyone is confronted with doomsday prophecies about the economy. People read about the shortcomings of the system and the decline of productivity; they see a frightening rate of unemployment, inflation, and default; and they find themselves in a socioeconomic system that functions with no particular direction, goals, or values. It is no wonder that they hesitate to invest. Why shouldn't their behavior reflect such dismal economic prospects?

The Need for New Expectations

We have developed the concept of government lending with the idea of creating an efficiently functioning economy based on full employment. We have at the same time dismissed the conventional theories, which foster the belief that unemployment and inflation are inevitable, and replaced them with monetary practices based on the assumption that full employment and a stable currency can be the foundations of a mature economy. It is our feeling that new expectations will develop out of the establishment of this system, and that people will react differently when they see that these expectations are being met.

Once we begin—once we take the first step toward full employment, a stable currency, and respect for human values —new and positive hopes will be created in people's minds. While the expectation of recession and a depressed economy certainly prevents corporate and private investors from making use of available credit, the expectation of a healthy economy will promote productive economic activity. If such ideals as responsibility, initiative, and creativity are incorporated into the economic system, these qualities will emerge in the individuals who make up this system.

In regard to the government, we should also bear in mind some problems that will require longer-range solutions than the ones mentioned here. We do not regard government lending merely as a technical credit operation. The concept of government lending carries with it the notion that we *need* a government and its help—a mature economy could not exist without a government. Yet we also need a government that will *serve* the economy, and not control it or take over activities better left to individuals or groups. The government has to be primarily a policymaking body and not an operating body. If we forget this, then the government will take over so many activities that it will become the employer of the nation instead of its servant.

Under a system of government lending, the government will have the duty of supplying the economy with sufficient means of payment but will not have the right to interfere on the level of business enterprise. It will be the banking system, and it will base its credit policy on commercial criteria. Nor will the government or any of its agencies have the right to tamper with the rate of interest—and particularly to use this tool as a brake on the development of the economy.

7
A
Stable
Price
Level

Prices and Purchasing Power

If we were to take a public-opinion poll on the question whether or not the government should be responsible for a stable currency, the majority of people would no doubt answer affirmatively. If we were to ask, "Who shall fix the prices of goods and services, the government or the market?" we would expect that most people would favor the market; few people want the prices of literally millions of items to be fixed by the government. Yet those who determine prices determine the stability or instability of the currency. This is so because an increase in prices creates a decrease in purchasing power, just as an increase in purchasing power amounts to a decrease in prices. From this it follows that an organization which has to establish a stable currency must actually stabilize prices.

Therefore, both answers to our hypothetical poll are correct: While the government *should* be responsible for the purchasing power of the means of payment that it issues— whether this takes the form of paper money or credit—it is also true that one should oppose a bureaucracy's power to fix prices. The enormous difficulties that government price-fixing has created in the Soviet Union support this claim. Furthermore, planned prices are part of a planned economy; introducing them into a mixed economy would result in even greater disaster. But if business enterprises fix prices, the relationship between purchasing power and prices—an increase in one leading to a decrease in the other—tells us that the government cannot be responsible for a stable currency.

Choosing the Lesser of Two Evils

It is certainly true that inflation is one of our worst economic problems—probably the worst of them all. Thus, stable purchasing power must be established and maintained. The difficulty is in determining whether government or business should be responsible for stabilization.

On the one hand, we know that if we permit business to stabilize purchasing power by fixing prices, we shall be encouraging the same evils we are trying to eliminate; this practice is largely responsible for our current economic crisis. On the other hand, from all that we have said concerning the government's responsibility to protect the economic rights of the consumer, it seems logical that the government should be responsible for stable purchasing power.

The Nature of Purchasing Power

Before turning to the specifics of price stabilization, let us examine the nature of purchasing power through a brief review of some of the ideas we have introduced in previous chapters: For as long as "commodity money" or gold-backed money has been in existence, the purchasing power of gold has actually been the purchasing power of gold-backed money. While the price, or exchange value, of gold fluctuated, for the most part it was reasonably stable and could be used as an economic barometer.

Suddenly, however, we had unbacked paper money. It had no inherent value, being simply a piece of paper with some legal backing that could be compared to a theater ticket. A theater ticket is a piece of paper protected by law. It has a price, or value, but only as a theater ticket: It is valuable because it entitles us to see a specific performance from a specific seat in a specific theater; it authorizes us to attend the performance. Without these entitlements, it is worthless. If someone forges it, he or she will be punished, and if a performance is canceled, the management refunds the money used to buy it.

Is Devaluation a Crime?

Actually, the protection given to an individual for paper money is far weaker than that for a theater ticket. As a rule, the entitlement, or value, of paper money is diminishing. It is as if a theater ticket suddenly entitled you to only part of a seat or to only the first act of a play. Theatergoers would find this ridiculous; they would sue the theater and stop buying tickets. Yet with money, something equally ridiculous is taken for granted, and even theoretically justified. Forging theater tickets is a crime because it lessens the value of the real product and cheats those entitled to a legitimate return. And yet when our money is worth less, when workers get a smaller return for their labor, no crime has been committed.

Prices Determine Purchasing Power

As long as our money was backed by a commodity such as gold, its purchasing power and the relative value of goods and services was determined by that commodity: money had purchasing power because it *represented* a commodity of value, and, since the value of gold was relatively stable, the gold standard served as a reliable measure of value for all goods and services and helped to stabilize prices. Once this commodity backing disappeared, however, money lost its inherent value and began to represent simply a unit of price— meaning that prices were expressed in monetary units.

In this situation, the purchasing power of money is determined by the prices of goods and services: when prices rise, purchasing power diminishes, because our money entitles us to fewer goods, services, and man-hours. Without the inherent value provided by commodity backing, money in itself has no purchasing power.

With this in mind, a closer look at how prices are determined may give us some clues as to how stable purchasing power can be achieved. Conventional economics textbooks teach us that a competitive market determines prices and so affects purchasing power, yet this interpretation is far too simplistic and misleading. For instance, wages and salaries, which make up the bulk of prices, are the result not of market forces but of conflicts and settlements between employers and employees. Similarly, the government's budgetary expenses are not determined by the market although they account for almost a third of the gross national product and half of household expenditures, and, as we have pointed out, the taxes used to finance the budget are projected into prices.

Unstable Purchasing Power Is Inherent

First of all, we must see that the government, which should guarantee stable prices, annually increases its expenditures, and so increases taxes to meet these expenditures. The higher taxes lead to tax increases and on to inflation. Thus, the government itself creates an economic system that is based not on stable prices but on a permanent increase in prices caused by its own uneconomical expenditures. As goods and services become more expensive because of the tax burden, the demand for higher wages naturally follows, and these higher rewards also increase prices. Once such a system exists, all too many people and enterprises will make use of its loopholes, and increase rewards and prices without increasing productivity.

We should bear in mind that approximately 50 percent of the price of consumer goods and services represents accumulated taxes, something more than 40 percent represents wages and salaries, and less than 10 percent represents pretax profit. (We do not deal in this context with the problem of imports.) Consequently, if we want stable prices, we must first of all insist that the government not expand its budget, and even reduce it if possible. Only then could we demand that wages and salaries increase according to the growth of productivity. The restriction on the budget's size could be achieved by government lending, replacing the practice of government spending for uneconomic purposes. Once prices did not rise owing to increased government expenditures, there would be no rational reason that an increase of wages without increased productivity should be demanded by the trade unions. After all, there is no way to increase *real* wages except by higher productivity: If we do increase wages without higher productivity, the increased wages will lead to increased prices, and what the workers gain in their paycheck they may lose to inflation. From this it follows that rewards would grow in relation to increased productivity, and prices would remain stable. The method to achieve this is profit-sharing, which we will deal with at length in Chapter 9.

Our economic system is also responsible for much of what business has been blamed for. A system based on stable prices forces business to be efficient, because profits won't be simply the result of increased prices but of better planning and organization and more efficient methods of production. If the economic system permits a business to increase its profits simply by increasing prices without concern for increased production or quality, however, the business will undoubtedly follow this course—the path of least resistance.

Prices MUST Be Stable

It is self-evident that the only way to prevent inflation and guarantee stable purchasing power is to concentrate on stabilizing the prices of goods and services. Prices must be stable; this is essential to efficient and productive economic functioning.

If we want to achieve stable prices within the framework of a free-enterprise system, we must go to the roots of price increases in our mature economy. We have already pointed out that accumulated taxes amount to something like 50 percent of the prices of consumer goods. The first step in stabilizing prices would be to stabilize government expenditures, and even to reduce them. After all, we cannot ask the government to stabilize market prices when the government itself, through its growing expenditures, is causing a large part of the price increases. We must avoid any increase in government expenditures and do everything we can to reduce them, and so reduce the final prices of goods and services.

Once government expenditures are no longer increasing and the self-evident economic principle that increased rewards must be dependent on increased productivity is applied, why should prices continue to rise? After all, the component of pretax profit is less than 10 percent of the price of a commodity; it would be no problem to maintain this level of profit and avoid price increases for profit reasons.

If productivity increases, so would profits. In our system, increased profit is the equivalent of increased productivity, and all those whose efforts helped achieve this increase should have a share. This part we call profit-sharing, and it should be the only increase of rewards. It would be an incentive to both workers and management in increasing productivity continuously.

In such a system, if a price ceiling was set, it would not be a mere administrative measure, as conventional (and never successful) wage and price ceilings are. To eliminate the causes of price increases by reducing government spending and introducing government lending is a most economic, and not an administrative, measure. Further, to state that an increase in wages should be an increase of real and not merely nominal wages is also an economic, and not administrative, measure. The concept of stable prices will therefore be basically an economic measure linked to profit-sharing—a measure that creates incentives for better performance.

Once stable prices have been established, the concept

of rewards, and particularly the concept of profit, will take on new meaning. Profit will be the result of increased effort, not increased prices, and this profit should not be whittled away by taxation. (We will deal with this idea in more detail in the next chapter.) Instead, it should be subject to profit-sharing, which we feel should become one of the most important components of a mature economy. Thus, increased productivity would be accompanied by an increase of rewards, and the growth of production would be followed by an increase in consumption, which would benefit the entire economy.

A New Role for Labor Unions

These new concepts of profit and reward will create a new role for labor unions and other organizations functioning in the realm of business. Management will have to become more concerned with increasing productivity in order to maximize profit. Labor unions will have to work hard to prevent increased productivity from becoming too much of a strain on their members, and, at the same time, will have to keep in mind that this productivity will also result in higher wages. A highly advanced technology enables us to produce more goods of better quality with less effort, and labor unions will certainly want to have this technology applied to the enterprises in which their members are employed. New methods of insuring job security will have to be developed, and the unions' interest in management science will increase so they can discover all the possibilities for making job security a reality. Certainly, the unions would not have the right to interfere with the management of the enterprises, but they could and should be prepared to ask for higher rewards and to present specific methods and programs through which these rewards could be achieved.

The new relationship between labor and management

may produce conflicts, but conflict is often fruitful in itself, and could become a common basis for cooperation. For example, if a business does not achieve high productivity and high profits, the workers could go on strike against the management and demand improved operations, because improved operations would give them more money through profit-sharing. Under such conditions, it would be in the interest of the shareholders and labor alike to pressure management to improve its performance.

At this point, it should be remembered that the fight for higher wages during the Industrial Revolution led to an increase in applied technology. Yet we should be aware that this happened at a time when gold and gold-backed money existed and prices were restrained by the existence of a stable price control. Today, when wage increases are automatically projected into prices, we face a vastly different situation, and labor organizations can no longer be concerned with their members simply as employees who need wage increases. Since these increases will be lost in a market that lacks stable purchasing power, unions must also see their members as consumers, and begin to involve themselves in the fight for stable prices.

Goods and the Competitive Market

One element of price stability that we have not yet considered is that of quality. The prices of goods and services are not merely nominal; they are, or should be, indicative of the quality of the goods or services in question. In fact, the quality of a commodity is closely related to its price. While the price of a pair of shoes might not change, it would still be relatively more expensive if its present quality declined. In stabilizing prices, we must also attempt to prevent the quality of goods and services from diminishing.

The effectiveness of bureaucratic measures is limited

in this regard. While the quality of such goods as medicine and food can be determined by standards and rules, as is the case at present, that of most of our commodities must be influenced and controlled by other, nonadministrative means, simply because of the difficulty of setting standards in such areas as taste and esthetics. The only effective way of doing this is on the market, through competition.

Unfortunately, as we know, the competitive power of the market, though it still exists, is anything but perfect. The growth and dominance of large corporate enterprises has drastically reduced competition and, in doing so, has caused the contemporary market to lose its original function and impetus. We are now confronted with the task of increasing competition to the market—of making it a buyer's rather than a producer's market. Our concern for consumers' rights requires that we focus primarily on the household market, which includes areas such as housing, public transportation, and those goods and services used by households. What is needed is a consumer group—a national institution, say—that will give consumers more of an opportunity to express their needs and desires and more influence to insure that their recommendations are acted upon wherever possible.

Since the government will control part of the credit supply under our new system, one method of achieving our goal will be to have the government use some earmarked credit to support small businesses so that they will be able to compete with large enterprises. Cooperative movements, central buying organizations, and supermarkets where small producers could sell their goods are some of the many methods that consumers themselves can introduce and control. Credit subsidies for small-scale production on an individual or cooperative basis would be the easiest and most effective way of fostering competition with large enterprises and could be done immediately.

Democratization of Price Control

There is always the danger, of course, that maintaining price stability could become the province of an administrative apparatus and so strengthen the bureaucracy. Therefore, other, more decentralized means of control should be sought. We have already mentioned the new role of trade unions in this regard, and a national consumer organization is certainly a possibility. In addition, town representatives, organizations of concerned citizens, and church and senior citizen groups could be assigned to watch over the price stability of goods and services most important to them, and to initiate corrective actions. The government's task would simply be to legalize and set norms for such organizations, to avoid arbitrariness and chaos. In this way, we could create an effective program for maintaining price stability with virtually no interference from government agencies.

We must also bear in mind that there is no need to control the prices of all goods and services. It is important to regulate the price level of commodities used primarily by lower-income and middle-income groups, but we do not have to be so concerned with luxury items and other products designed for those with large incomes. Furthermore, our task is facilitated by the stabilization of the prices of final goods, rather than that of the elements used to produce these goods. This is because the price of the end product limits the prices of its components. Finally, we should realize that if we cease to cause and justify price increases and inflation, and, in fact, begin to think of them as crimes, we shall create a new economic climate that will help prevent practices causing monetary instability.

Problems in Price Stability

Thus far, we have dealt with the attempt to stabilize purchasing power by focusing on the price control of domestic goods. At this point, we must consider the problems created by the price fluctuations of imported goods, particularly raw materials, and by the uncontrolled prices of new products on the market. How is it possible to avoid their potentially inflationary impact?

We have already witnessed a fourfold increase in the price of imported oil and seen its adverse effects on the productive process of nations such as the United States. The current solution to this problem is to reduce the country's dependence on foreign oil. In addition, although the cost of domestic production did not change and the proportion of imported oil was not too large, the increased cost of imported oil has been accepted for oil produced domestically. This reflects the concept of unstable prices.

In an economy that insists on price stability, programs that would prevent price increases of imported commodities from upsetting a nation's price structure would have to be developed. In the case of imported oil, we must keep in mind that a price increase of a dollar a barrel creates a chain reaction domestically that will result in price increases of three, four, or more dollars in a great number of products made from oil or petroleum derivatives. Stable prices can be maintained *only* if such increases are prohibited.

One way of maintaining price stability in such cases might be to create a special fund out of which the difference between the original import price and the new, "blackmail" price would be paid. This special fund might be created through a "skimming" sales tax—one that makes it possible to increase the sales tax, say, on certain luxury items but not the prices of goods and services bought by the less affluent. The burden would fall on those who are more able to afford it, the general price level would remain the same, and there would be no inflationary demand for higher wages. Through a consumer subsidy of this type, oil could be sold on the home market at the original price.

As for new commodities, we do not think that they would create a problem of great magnitude. The price of such relatively new products as color television sets and small computers have, in fact, been declining as their production has grown.

Objections

The opponents of price stabilization claim that measures such as we have proposed would have an adverse effect upon production and the market; stable prices would cause manufacturers to stop producing, they say, and the resulting shortage of goods would automatically create either inflation or a black market. Such reasoning seems illogical to us. If goods and services are produced at a given price level, why should production suddenly stop when prices are stabilized at that level?

Actually, because inflation has a great tendency to inhibit investment and production, the assumption that production would *increase* in a stable economic environment is quite reasonable. Furthermore, our program involves only the fixing of prices, not of rewards. We do not assume that wages and any kinds of rewards should be fixed. On the contrary, we advocate higher rewards through higher productivity, which would be a great incentive to increase both the quantity and quality of goods and services produced.

The Ethics of Stable Prices

Up until now, we have been speaking of price stability primarily from an economic point of view. But the absolute necessity of creating a stable price level and the impact of this stability on the entire socioeconomic system far transcends purely economic considerations. Once prices are stabilized, profit will take on a perfectly new connotation: It will become the reward for better performance, and its role as an incentive for efficient and productive work will be enhanced, particularly when we begin to think of it in the context of profit-sharing, where rewards are given to all who have a share in the productive process.

Profit has been introduced into all economic systems, including the planned economies of the Soviet model. Experience has shown that no economy can function without the existence of the material incentives profit provides. It might be argued that certain groups have established communes with functioning economies based on higher ideals than material gain. These communal economic systems are exceptions, however; they are composed of relatively small numbers of people whose motive, it is true, is other than profit, but they cannot be considered typical of a developed economy.

In practically all contemporary economic systems, monetary incentives are recognized as being of the utmost importance. Without incentives, employees and employers would have little or no concern for their own performance.

Financial incentives for the owners of the means of production are usually called profit, and the necessity for profit is recognized by most people. It is, at the same time, seen as a necessary evil (often with more emphasis on the "evil" than on the "necessary"). It is important to realize that particularly with big corporations there are incentives other than profit—status, power, prestige. Still, profit remains the decisive incentive.

Being concerned with human dimensions in a mature economy, one based on the Judeo-Christian philosophy, we must ask whether profit has its place in the economy we envision. In our view, profit should be the reward for the services rendered to the people. The task is how to project this ethical concept into economic categories. First of all, profit must not be the result of increased prices, and also wages should not increase without higher productivity. Either of these situations, if allowed, would result in higher prices, as we have explained. If prices were stabilized in this manner, wages or profits could not be increased simply by forcing the consumer to pay more. Under conditions of stable prices, profit as well as wages will be the result of more efficient business performance. Having this in mind, we find it fair that all who have a part in the improved performance of the economy must have a share in the profit. Thus, stable prices plus profit-sharing gives the concept of profit new ethical dimensions. Profit would be a reward for producing a bigger cake, and at the same time the shares of the cake for the workers would increase as well.

In a system where arbitrary increases in the prices of labor, goods, and services are the sources of profit, the society and the economy can be termed virtually immoral; the "form of ownership" is irrelevant in this situation. Thus, the establishment of stable prices and a system of profit-sharing not only serves as a solution to economic and monetary problems but also contributes to solving social and human problems.

We can go further in our discussion of the social, rather than economic, implications of establishing stable prices by considering the effects of price stability on the three factors that we feel have contributed the most to the successful development of individuals and nations. These are initiative, responsibility, and creativity.

Initiative

We view the economy and the society as a system of thinking human beings, and we therefore place great emphasis on *initiative*. When people will feel that their initiative is appreciated, they will be apt to make use of their ability to think, to innovate, to invent, to be more concerned with their work. While in planned economies a preoccupation with target figures leaves little room for initiative, the freedom of a mixed economy allows initiative to take many forms. Initiative is not in itself necessarily good; it must be judged on the basis of human values. So we have to provide safeguards against using initiative only for one's own benefit without regard for the well-being of others. A system in which prices can be manipulated to the consumer's disadvantage, or in which profit is increased at the whole nation's expense, does not encourage the kind of initiative we wish to see developed, because it does not serve the needs of others.

By introducing stable prices and changing the conventional concepts of reward and profit, we shall be moving toward the establishment of a socioeconomic system in which a positive and beneficial form of initiative will be fostered. Because increased rewards for both businesses and employees will result only from new and more efficient methods of production, a new concern on the part of management and labor for promoting better and more productive working conditions will be developed. This new initiative in the business realm will also expand into that of the consumers, who, realizing that their activity through newly created consumer organizations is appreciated, will increase their efforts to protect the consumer rights of the entire nation.

Responsibility

What we are saying here is, of course, closely tied to the element of responsibility. Certainly, systems based on an absolute concentration of economic power such as the Soviet model do little to promote responsibility among the citizens of a nation. Such a system is set up so that all responsibility is in the hands of a powerful elite, whose members, being above criticism from the rest of the population, are responsible only to themselves. In contrast, the programs and methods we are recommending are designed to place the responsibility for a fully functioning and efficient economy on the workers and consumers of the nation. The ideal is to create a society in which every organization and institution is based and structured on the principle of responsibility.

Although individual responsibility is one of the basic values of Western civilization, our society does little to promote the spirit and content of these values. What kind of responsibility can exist in a system where increased rewards are possible without any increase in the quantity and quality of goods and services? Such increases are, in fact, totally counterproductive. Not only are they deceptive, in that workers who get such increased rewards quickly lose them as consumers, but the effects of such practices are also demoralizing, because people will feel not that their increased contribution to the wealth of the nation is being rewarded but that they get increased wages or salaries for their militancy or that of their organization. They will be even more alienated from true labor, feeling that it is not their labor but other factors that lead to an increase in wages. In short, rewards have to be rewards for accomplishment, so employees will have the feeling that their work is appreciated by and has meaning for the society.

In a system that bestows rewards for the wrong reasons, responsibility and initiative are being replaced by mediocrity —and this to such a degree that responsibility and initiative are rarely even encouraged or respected. We must begin to question the orientation of such a system and to determine whether or not our society and economy are fostering initiative and responsibility. It makes a tremendous difference whether our system permits them to flourish or to be dominated by selfishness, ambivalence, and mediocrity. The introduction of stable prices and the other measures and concepts we are suggesting will, as we have said, encourage elements that lead to a more humane and productive economic system.

Irresponsible Welfare

A classic example of the ways in which the current system undermines responsibility and initiative can be found in the practice of social welfare. While we consider the concept of welfare for those in need to be essentially a good one, its impact on our society is potentially quite harmful. When welfare payments are supplied by the government simply to please the voting public, productive work is degraded. The incentive to work and to use one's initiative and act in a responsible manner is reduced, because, as the many people "on welfare" have discovered, the difference between welfare benefits and wages, the actual reward for work, is often relatively small. The welfare system should express the responsibility of the society toward those who need public assistance but should demand that those who have the opportunity and ability to care for themselves do so and not burden the society.

Furthermore, while it is generally believed that the financial burden welfare creates is being carried primarily by the government, the business enterprises, and the wealthy, this is a misconception. Since the welfare system is financed by taxes, and taxes are projected into prices, *it is actually* the consumer who pays. Here again we are confronted with the lack of responsibility of those who allow such misconceptions to exist and who support a system that degrades productive work. In addition, the impression that the government pays for such benefits creates a climate of passivity and a lack of initiative and responsibility. Citizens begin to feel that they can afford to be passive because their "big brother," the government, will do everything for them, and so they tend to put more and more responsibility on the government. This increases an already overburdened and inefficient bureaucracy.

Creativity

In these and many other ways, the economic system also limits the potential effects of the element of creativity, which goes hand in hand with initiative and responsibility. As a matter of fact, one of the most creative components of our society, the business-enterprises realm, is being blamed for our economic ills these days. In the search for a scapegoat, we witness price increases and job layoffs carried out by business enterprises, and accuse them of disrupting our economy; yet we remain unaware of the forces that make them act as they do.

We must begin to realize that outdated monetary theories and practices and the ineffective science of economics on which the government relies are at the root of our problems. Unfortunately, this is not so easy to understand, and the real culprit escapes the blame that is its due.

As long as we continue to use these theories and concepts, we shall continue to promote a socioeconomic system that inhibits, rather than encourages, creative thinking and action. Truly creative individuals may represent a minority in our society; still, this minority must have the opportunity to function freely or we will not receive the social and economic benefits that they can offer us.

Conventional economic practices are sustaining a system that has little room for individual and corporate creativity, initiative and responsibility. Unless we allow the creative minority to be free and responsible for their creation, we shall witness the destruction of those forces which form the basis of our hopes for a successful society in the future. Even a few small steps toward orienting our economy in this direction will give us the feeling that we can control the economy, that we can create our own future, and that we shall be the subjects of history and not its objects.

8
Outdated
Taxation

The Unquestioned Philosophy

"The state needs money to pay its bills. It gets this money primarily from taxes." This textbook explanation of taxation is not only the common philosophy on which taxation is based but also the most generally accepted explanation of and justification for the payment of taxes. Almost everyone dislikes paying taxes; many try to reduce their taxes through loopholes and deductions, some try to avoid paying altogether, and others attempt to reform the tax system. With all these different approaches to taxation, however, the actual concept of taxation remains unquestioned; everyone believes that the government *does* need money to pay its bills and that the nation *should* pay taxes.

We see how this principle operates in practice, and how the philosophy of taxation becomes frightening. Year after year, the government is in need of more money, because it has more bills to pay. Already these bills amount to a third of the gross national product. Forty to fifty cents out of every dollar paid by consumers for the great majority of goods and services can be traced to the taxes projected into the prices of these commodities.

The More We Pay, the Less We Get

In spite of the fact that we individuals pay a fantastic amount of money in taxes, and are consequently poorer, a large proportion of our tax dollars is spent on programs and activities from which we receive no benefit. We can assume that if this money was used for productive purposes, we might benefit more from our payments, but the fact of the matter is that we pay more and receive less as time goes on.

The Unmanageable Bureaucracy

Ever-increasing numbers of the nation's tax dollars are used to fund the bureaucracy. Every level of government is being entrusted with more and more tasks and responsibilities, and administrative costs are constantly increasing. Politicians hoping to gain votes make promises that increase the burden carried by local and national governments and simply present the bill to the people. This practice enhances an already cumbersome bureaucracy's inefficiency and increases its power. Before they know it, both the citizens and the politicians responsible for the bureaucracy's growth are confronted with a bureaucratic system so powerful it is out of their control.

That this is possible is often difficult to understand, but the nature of a bureaucracy makes such consequences likely. Actually, the single bureaucrat has little power. Regardless of whether or not he likes the rules of the system, he is obligated to follow them; he has a responsibility and must live up to it. The bureaucratic system as a whole, however, is quite powerful, and could accurately be compared to a piece of rope: although the individual strands of this rope (like the individual bureaucrat) are weak and easily torn, when bound into a rope (the bureaucratic system) they cannot be broken. The bigger the bureaucracy, the more strict and numerous are the rules and regulations necessary. The Internal Revenue Service, employing some 200,000 people, has issued more than 20,000 regulations of various kinds. Unfortunately, the taxes used to "pay the bills of the nation" contribute to the power of a bureaucratic system that makes the ordinary citizen, the politician, and even the government helpless. Some of the consequences of government spending mentioned above are important in this regard: An increase in government spending means a growth of the scope of government activity, and this leads to increased government power, and to a more autonomous and powerful bureaucracy. At present, we cannot command the power of the bureaucratic apparatus that we ourselves have created.

Questioning the Unquestioned Philosophy

We do not suggest that taxation should be eliminated. We realize that our complex socioeconomic system could not exist without a centralized government, and that the government must have money to function. What disturbs us is that the current philosophy of taxation simply states that the government needs money to pay *its* bills and that the nation has no choice but to supply the needed funds.

Forced Labor or Free Labor

It could logically be stated that in order for our socioeconomic system to function, the citizenry must work. But if we accept the notion that we *must* work so the system can function, we are actually accepting a system of forced labor. If we were to protest against such a system, it would not mean that we feel we should not have to work but only that we wish to work as free citizens, and at jobs that have meaning for us. Our protest would actually be directed against the fact that the government has the power to force us to work. Our desire would be to create a system in which the opportunity to work was provided but not forced upon us. The question is not whether to work or not to work, but whether the system, the government, will command us or serve us.

This same logic applies to taxation. The existing philosophy for taxation is similar to that of forced labor: It gives the government the right to spend and *forces* the citizens to pay. Instead of this, we would propose a system in which the government serves the nation instead of commanding it. The bills are actually the bills of the nation, and, because of this, the nation must have the right to decide the scope and structure of the expenditures—to pay its own bills, not the government's.

Who Really Pays the Taxes?

The problem, of course, is how to make our proposed system a reality and, in doing so, to eliminate the unfortunate consequences of the current system. Before we turn to the solution to this problem, however, let us consider the question of who actually pays the bills.

It is clear that corporate taxes make up part of the prices of consumer goods. Consequently, although the corporation technically pays its own taxes, the consumer is actually the taxpayer in this case. Also, it is obvious that the consumer supplies state and local governments with funds through the sales tax on certain goods and services. Far less obvious is who pays the income tax.

At first glance, it would seem that income taxes are paid by those who get the income. Although in some cases, as with inheritance taxes, this is certainly true, the reality of the situation is different as far as most of the nation's income is concerned. All wages consist of net wages *plus* income taxes, and since these wages are part of the prices of goods and services, the consumer is actually paying the bulk of the nation's income tax. When we add this to the payment of corporate taxes and state sales taxes, we are confronted with the shocking fact that the consumer is paying approximately 90 percent or more of all the taxes paid to the government.

Equally important is the fact that the great majority of consumers are completely unaware of how great a tax burden they carry. They do not realize that approximately 50 percent of each dollar they spend goes toward taxes of one form or another. Yet they should know this. They should be aware of the fact that they are the ones who pay the bills, and that they have the right to decide how their money is to be spent.

It follows from this that when consumers are made aware that they pay the bulk of taxes, they will become more concerned with what they are paying for, and will not accept the rationale that the government must pay its bills while they simply pay the taxes. They will then realize that the conventional philosophy of taxation is *more the expression of a power relationship between the government and the people than simply the fact of payment;* that a system in which the government has the right to spend and the consumer the duty to pay is all too similar to a system of forced labor.

Democracy, Taxation, and Spending

In contrast to these ideas, it could be argued that taxation is justifiable because it operates in a democratic society. In this system, it is the representatives of the nation who decide how the taxpayer's money is to be spent; in other words, the nation decides on this matter through its elected officials. While we cherish the fact that a democratic system grants people the right to express their views in elections, we should not overestimate the effectiveness of this system.

We must keep in mind that the current concept of taxation is closely tied to a belief in the benefits of government spending. This belief tends to encourage the government to take on more and more tasks and responsibilities. As a result, we place a tremendous financial burden on the taxpayer who has to pay the bill, and, in addition, we create a tremendous bureaucracy, inefficient by its very nature and extremely powerful. While all this takes place through democratic processes, the chaotic situation that results is certainly not what the nation had intended.

The fiscal crisis in New York City, the most important city in the United States and the world, is a perfect example of this. There, democratically elected officials were entrusted with certain tasks to be paid for through government spending, and large amounts of money were required because the city government needed money to pay its bills. Regardless of the noble intentions of the people of New York and their representatives, bureaucratic inefficiency nearly resulted in bankruptcy, and caused the closing of schools, hospitals, and libraries, a cutback in essential services, and a general decline in the quality of life there.

While free election of a nation's representatives is the natural basis for any democratic system, we must also be concerned with the programs of democracy as well. With regard to the economy, this would mean that the nation must pay *its own* bills, and must decide not only who its representatives shall be but also how much it will pay for whatever services and responsibilities it passes on to the government. This principle is to be seen as an attempt to expand political democracy to the economic realm by making the government serve the socioeconomic system according to the democratically expressed will of the nation.

The "Social Contract"

For a better understanding of how this concept would be applied in practice, and to further explain our new ideas regarding taxation, let us begin to discuss how these ideas can be incorporated into the economic system described in the previous chapters. We have been speaking of a democratic society that should encompass economic as well as political democracy. We pointed out in the previous chapter that in the system we envision, the nation would vote on a program as well as the politicians responsible for fulfilling this program. Not only would a candidate's or party's program be a campaign issue but, in expanding political democracy to the economic realm, the estimated cost, or budget, for implementing a program would also become an election issue. Thus, the election of an individual or a party to office takes the form of a *social contract:* in taking office, the chosen politicians are obligated to carry out their program and to do so within the proposed budget.

The Fulfillment of the Social Contract

Suppose you contract a construction firm to build a house. By means of your personal check, the builder is given a specified amount of credit to pay for the cost of building the home. In the unlikely event that the contractor fails to build the house, the credit received for the house must be returned. But normally when the construction firm delivers the house it was contracted to build, the credit is repaid through the fulfillment of the contract. Under our new system, such an economic relationship would exist between the nation and the government.

In this situation, the people of a nation are like the family that orders the house. It gives credit to the builder—the government—and this credit is repaid when the government delivers the house, the program that it has promised; thus, the social contract is fulfilled. It is important to remember that the government should not be seen as external to the nation or to the economy. The philosophy of democracy mandates that the government be an organ of the nation and a part of the socioeconomic system. When the government is given the right to create the amount of credit specified in the budget, it has no obligation other than to fulfill the social contract under which it was elected; its credit does not have to be repaid.

Superfluous Purchasing Power

It should be obvious that the credit spent by the government in paying the salaries of its employees, purchasing weapons, buildings, and spacecraft, and generally fulfilling its part of the contract, will eventually become part of the total credit supply we have spoken about. Let us suppose that the dollar value of the goods and services produced and sold for household consumption amounts to $600 billion for a single year. In addition, let us say that the government's budgeted credit amounts to $300 billion, which finds its way into the market in the form of checks for wages, goods, and services. Thus, with the money spent by the government added to the nation's existing personal income, we find ourselves with superfluous means of payments of $300 billion—the budgetary expenditures.

This superfluous purchasing power would be most harmful to the economy; it would be as if a theater sold more tickets to a performance than it had seats available. Because great attempts have been made to introduce and maintain stable prices in our new system, it would be only logical to expect that a black market would develop, charging higher prices for certain goods, and, at the very least, that a great loss of faith in the currency would result. Large numbers of people would lose their purchasing power, for there would be too much money available and not enough goods and services on which to spend it.

If such a situation existed, we would expect that the nation would exercise its democratic rights and demand that the government do something to *take away* this superfluous purchasing power. In responding to this demand, the government would have to develop some way of *skimming off* this extra $300 billion. The nation would not merely say that the government has paid its bills and that we must now pay our taxes; instead, it would realize that there are more means of payment than goods and services available, and, because this situation is unhealthy for the economy, it would ask the government to skim off the superfluous money.

Skimming and Its Implications

In essence, this "skimming" would involve the government's requiring that a specified rate of skimming would be charged on all goods and services purchased by consumers; the rate of skimming would be collected in much the same way that the sales tax is collected now. Assuming that the amount of taxes currently projected into prices accounts for 50 percent of each dollar spent, when taxes are eliminated, prices would be reduced by 50 cents per dollar. In order to prevent superfluous purchasing power from endangering the economy, the government would charge this same 50 cents per dollar as the rate of skimming.

At this stage, everyone would protest that all we have done is to change the way taxes are collected. Taxation has not really been eliminated; instead, we seem to have simply replaced income tax, corporate tax, and sales tax with a larger sales tax, and to have changed the name from "taxation" to "skimming." However, although the impact of skimming would not be felt by the consumer initially, we maintain that the difference between the conventional form of taxation and that of skimming taxation is of primary importance, and that this practice will affect both the consumer and the economy in many different and beneficial ways.

We will have eliminated a system in which the government has become an all-powerful institution that simply spends money and then forces the nation to pay. Under our new system, the consumer will be very much aware that he must pay 50 cents on every dollar he spends and will consequently be quite concerned with what this 50 cents is being used for. We shall create a new climate of concern for the economic well-being of the nation.

We must realize that the rate of skimming will depend primarily on the size of the government's budget. Since any reduction in the budget will reduce the scope of skimming taxes, a healthy pressure will be created to minimize the scope of the government's activities and to restrict the growth of a counterproductive bureaucracy. If, for example, a politician wished to propose some costly new program for the government, he would first have to deal with how this program would affect the rate of skimming. The nation's citizens would have to consider carefully whether this new program would be worth the resulting increase in the skimming rate. Because it is the consumer who will be the most affected by any changes in the rate of skimming, it will be to his advantage to take the responsibility for insuring that such pressure is maintained, and, through increased political consciousness and action, to inhibit, rather than encourage, the financial irresponsibility of which New York City's fiscal crisis is a frightening example.

This new concern for economic well-being will be further enhanced by the fact that economic productivity and growth also contribute to a reduction in the skimming type of tax. A growing economy requires an increase in existing means of payments—that is, in the credit supply. In a fully functioning economy, it can be reasonably expected that the credit supply will have to expand by 4 to 5 percent a year, and this would mean that we would have to skim off that much less, because an increase in products will reduce the amount of superfluous money that has to be skimmed off. The skimming tax could be reduced by this same 4 or 5 percent and the consumer would have to pay 2 to 2.5 cents less than the usual 50 cents per dollar. Thus, skimming involves far more than simply giving taxation another name.

Advantages Over the Present System

Other advantages to the introduction of skimming are found in its replacement of conventional methods of taxation, which are far more unjust and inefficient. First of all, skimming would virtually eliminate the possibility of tax evasion through tax loopholes or shelters. The current system of tax deduction would thus become meaningless, and would be abandoned. Furthermore, the ease with which skimming taxes, in the form of sales taxes, could be implemented, and the comparatively simple methods of checking the payment of the skimming taxes would greatly increase the efficiency and effectiveness of administrative bodies such as the United States Internal Revenue Service and reduce their numbers, if they continued to exist at all.

A tremendous amount of money could be saved by eliminating the large losses in revenue caused by tax evasion and deduction and through the increased efficiency of the collection system. These savings would naturally be passed on to the consumer in the form of further reductions in the rate of skimming. More important, however, the nation would no longer be confronted with the fact that some millionaires pay less in taxes than the average citizen, and one important element of tax immorality would be disposed of.

The End of Interest on Government Debts

Today, 9 or 10 percent of the government's budget goes for interest on money borrowed by the government—the so-called national debt. Government debts are the result of conventional budgetary practices and inefficient methods of taxation, which force the government to come to the marketplace, borrow, and then pay interest on the loan. The government borrows in the same way that a corporation or an individual borrows, but when it comes to the payment of interest, the government suddenly changes its role and asks the nation to pay its bills. This practice, which keeps the government's budget and our taxes high, would be eliminated under a system in which skimming was used.

If we accept conventional monetary theories and concepts, and therefore, payment by money, then the government is forced to go to the market to borrow, and is forced to pay interest, the cost of which is passed on to the consumer through taxes. But in an economic system based on credit supply rather than money supply, with a government financing its operation through credit in the manner we have suggested, there would be no reason for the government to go into debt, and certainly none to pay interest on that debt. The interest component would be eliminated, the government's budget would be reduced, another tax burden would be lifted from the consumer, and a further reduction in skimming taxes would be possible.

Restructuring Purchasing Power

In our discussion, we have thus far maintained a fixed rate of skimming for all commodities. Yet there is no reason why the rate should be the same. By introducing the idea that the rate of skimming can vary from one commodity to another, we would introduce a new tool for controlling prices.

It is generally known, for example, that there are different "consumer baskets" for different income groups—the members of a given income group generally restrict their spending to a certain range of items. This is not to say that a lower-income worker does not ever buy luxury goods, or that a millionaire never buys a commodity common to a lower-income basket. But thorough studies that have been made give us a general idea of how much will be spent on which goods and services by a family at a given income level. With this knowledge, it is certainly possible to structure the rate of skimming to redistribute income more equally.

On the one hand, goods and services bought mainly by lower-income groups—most of the mass-produced or essential commodities and services—could be given a low, or even a *negative rate* of skimming. (A negative skimming rate would involve some form of price subsidy.) On the other hand, luxury and semiluxury items could be burdened with skimming taxes far higher than the average of 50 cents per dollar. As a result, we would be able to achieve a remarkable redistribution of income. A worker of average income would spend 20 to 30 cents less per dollar for the items he buys now, because those items would be burdened with a low skimming tax. And the items in the consumer basket of those in high-income groups would be burdened with a skimming tax of 60 to 70 cents per dollar. Thus the real income—and that is what actually matters—would increase among low-income workers and decline among high-income groups.

The rate of skimming could also be varied according to criteria other than that of income. Healthy food could have a lower skimming rate than commodities such as alcohol and tobacco. The rent for low- or middle-income housing or apartments could have much lower rates than luxury apartments or estates. Skimming could also be used to support anti-pollution controls in automobiles and factories, and the production of goods made of recycled materials, as well as innumerable other products that affect human beings and their environment. Shopkeepers and other small businesspeople and producers would be able to remain in a market that has increasingly become more dominated by big business if the rate of skimming applied to their products helped keep their prices competitive.

Skimming as a Democratic Tool

The concept of a variable skimming tax is a fantastic tool through which the nation can effectively redirect the orientation of its economy toward goals of its own choosing. And in redirecting the economy it is most important that we take full advantage of its potential for making the concept of economic democracy—where all the people will have a voice—a reality. By permitting the skimming rate and its specific applications to be matters for public discussion and voting, we can increase the people's role in economic decision-making, and democracy can be expanded to the economic realm. Through the democratic use of this tool, we can not only improve the standard of living for the underprivileged but also improve the quality of life of the entire nation.

Taxation, Free Enterprise, Efficient Production

Although the free-enterprise system is related to the idea that the government should not directly interfere with the performance of individual businesses, such interference exists and is, in fact, permissible through current taxation practices. Furthermore, while taxation is actually a means of nationalizing profit, those who oppose all forms of nationalization and of government interference simultaneously accept these practices through taxation. Not only does taxation restrict freedom of enterprise but the effect of taxation upon business is so great that it has become a consideration in many of the major decisions made by corporate administrators; this is especially true with regard to investment policy and other areas indirectly controlled by laws and procedures established by government tax agencies.

As a means of demonstrating how taxation practices can affect business enterprises, let us consider two enterprises that produce the same commodities and charge the same price for their products. Under the conventional system of taxation, this price reflects the profits expected from the sale of these commodities and the taxes to be paid on the profits. While one of the enterprises is more efficient, makes a profit, and must pay taxes, the other enterprise, because of poor management and inefficient production practices, shows a loss and pays no tax. Since the prices of its goods include the taxes that the less efficient enterprise expected to pay to the government, this enterprise's losses were kept at a minimum. Not only was it the consumer who paid for these losses but the more efficient enterprise was penalized for its efficiency through taxation. Unless the efficient company resorts to illegal tax loopholes and deductions, the more profit it makes through efficiency, the more taxes it will pay. Particularly if we introduce profit-sharing, this type of taxation must be abolished. Those who contributed to a profit would actually be punished. Therefore, it is important to exempt both corporations as well as labor from taxes.

In this and many other ways, current taxation practices restrict freedom of enterprise and inhibit the productive capacity of the economy. We might also add in this regard, that one method the government uses to increase economic activity is that of lowering taxes, implying that taxes *do* have a damping effect on business activity at both the corporate and consumer levels. That the damage done to the economy by taxation is far greater than the benefits accruing from it would not be difficult to prove. Consequently, we propose to abandon conventional tax procedures and to replace them with tax skimming—an alternative that will provide many benefits for the economy and the society as a whole.

Is Skimming Regressive?

In contrast to all we have said concerning the benefits of skimming, it could be argued that taxation solely by means of a sales tax is a regressive practice. What is meant by regressive is that, in a situation where the income tax has been eliminated and all taxes are paid through a levy on the sale of goods and services, those with higher incomes would be far better off than those with lower incomes; since the tax would be the same for all groups, the higher-income group could better afford to pay the tax.

Keeping in mind the many advantages of skimming over conventional tax procedures, we have attempted to deal with this problem by structuring the rate of skimming according to the consumer baskets of different income groups. If the consumer basket of a family earning $10,000 a year was given a rate of 10 cents per dollar, and that of a family earning

$100,000 a year a rate of 60 cents for every dollar spent, and, in addition, each family spent its entire income, the higher-income family would pay approximately $60,000 in "skimmed income," while the family with less income would pay only slightly more than $1,000. In other words, through structured skimming, higher-income families would have two-thirds of their income skimmed while lower-income families would pay only one-tenth of theirs. It could still be argued that this safeguard would be ineffective if higher-income families were satisfied with products belonging to the consumer basket of lower-income groups; these families could conceivably save $90,000 "tax free"—void of skimming.

At this point in our discussion, we seem to have reached an impasse. If we abolish taxes, we must naturally abolish personal-income taxes along with all other forms of taxation. But without the equalizing effect of the personal-income tax, how shall we insure the fair redistribution of income that we feel is both a political, social, ethical, and economic necessity?

The Social Share

The answer lies in the concept of the social share. It is our feeling that, in view of the social structure of our economic system, which is characterized by an arbitrary and unjust distribution of income, it is necessary for the higher-income groups to give a share of their income toward the maintenance of the social well-being of their nation. We would advise that a social share be introduced which would take the form of a progressive income tax. The social share would be used specifically for certain agreed upon tasks and programs that would serve to benefit the majority of the nation. Although the concept of the social share would resemble that of the personal-income tax in practice, the difference between them is great.

We have already pointed out that the corporate income tax as it exists today is actually paid primarily by the consumer, since this tax is figured into the prices of goods and services. As a result, the consumer, whether rich or poor, ends up paying the personal-income tax of the employer and the employees of the corporation whose commodity he buys, and even a person on welfare ends up returning a part of his welfare check by paying the tax component of the price. The concept of the social-share tax would eliminate this obvious injustice and enable lower-income groups to benefit from a new type of personal-income tax rather than suffering because of the old one. Some of the areas in which social-share funds could be used would be child care, help for the aged, public-health and educational services, research grants, environmental programs and controls, and programs supporting the arts, literature, and public television.

Social Share, Efficiency, Economic Democracy

From the point of view of the income earner, there would appear to be no obvious difference between the conventional income tax and the social-share sort of tax. Yet the essential difference is tremendous. Income tax goes into the common budget and can be used for any purpose. It need not be used in the development of our economy as a whole, nor does it contribute to a redistribution of income; and it is instrumental in increasing the scope of a bureaucracy that is as inefficient as it is costly.

The social-share type of tax is *not* to be channeled into the general budget. Two separate sets of tasks would have to be met out of this income—one direct, the other indirect, and both helping to redistribute income. The indirect task would be to support cultural activities, museums, libraries, adult education—areas that would offer to all citizens more possibilities for meeting their cultural and spiritual needs. The other set of tasks would have the character of direct help. Money would go to support care for children, to improve health and living conditions, and, generally, to increase the living standard of those in need who are not able to help themselves through their own efforts. This would be a real distribution of wealth; everybody who has to contribute must have the right to know where his or her money goes.

In all these activities, the government's role will be limited to issuing only legislative or other norms. The institutions or agencies thus established by law to administer the programs will have representatives from trade unions, churches, ethical organizations, organizations of interested citizens, and particularly organizations of senior citizens, who represent a growing new social stratum with great potential.

Further, we assume that the scope and structure of activities that are supposed to be covered out of the social-share income could and should become election issues. So would the structure of the tax: In other words, what each income group's share should be. Thus we would expand democracy into our socioeconomic life.

Aside from the specific benefits that will result from a redistribution of income in this way, the simple act of decentralization will do much to improve the efficiency of the government. If a large enough number of activities for which the central government has always been responsible can be controlled at lower levels, the government's budget will decrease, and the lowered rate of skimming that will result will benefit consumers throughout the nation. Bureaucratic efficiency will be enhanced as fiscal and administrative responsibility for social-share programs is taken up by business enterprises, banks, or newly formed citizen groups. Furthermore, the concept of economic democracy can easily be incorporated into the administration of social share, for questions involving the earmarking of funds, the choice of programs, and the structuring of what portion of the social share shall be paid by whom will have to be matters of public discussion and election.

Skimming and the Soviet Sales Tax

The sales tax is the prevailing form of taxation in the Soviet economic system; the income tax exists, but it is of far less importance. With this in mind, one could assume that the system we have introduced here is an adaptation of the Soviet model designed for mixed economies. The essence of skimming is completely different from the sales tax in the Soviet Union, however, as well as from that in our own system. In the economic system we propose, *the principle of skimming is meant to widen the scope of democracy to include the economic realm, to be a tool through which a democratic government can carry out programs that have been democratically approved by the nation as a whole, and finally, to facilitate the functioning of a democratizing and humanizing socioeconomic system.* In the Soviet system, the role of the sales tax is this: An enterprise bases its prices essentially on costs plus overhead. Yet the government, as sole owner of all enterprises, has its own overhead. The government pays for investments, for research, for development, as well as for the usual government expenditures. The sales tax covers practically all the expenditures of the government—the absolute political and economic monopolist. The sales tax is thus one of the oppressive weapons of the dictatorship, and serves no other purpose.

Often, when we speak of "money" or "credit" or "taxes," we assume that the concepts the words represent can be accurately applied to the East in the same way that they are used in the West. Unfortunately, this is not the case; the differences between these concepts as they function in their separate systems could not be greater.

In the Soviet model or any other type of planned economy, one can use money or credit to buy only what has been produced within the national economic plan and has been allocated for the consumer. Soviet consumers cannot buy

132

tractors, trucks, or machines; these are produced specifically for the nationalized industries, and money has no purchasing power with regard to such commodities. Money in this planned economy functions as a combination of ration cards and what we think of as money. It goes without saying that no Soviet citizen can buy shares in an enterprise.

This difference in concepts also applies to prices and taxation. In order to understand these concepts and how they function in the Soviet economy, one has to bear in mind again that the means of production of the entire country—industry, agriculture, banks, radio, television, newspapers, publishing companies, everything—belongs to a single owner: the government, the operating body of the Politburo. Organs of this monopolistic owner fix the prices of all goods and services, and they do so absolutely arbitrarily.

The government's control of prices in the Soviet Union applies to all commodities at every level of production. Prices are assigned to raw materials, semiraw materials, and, in the end, to the final product. These prices are to be understood as the planned costs of production, and to these production costs the government adds its own overhead, or profit. It is not called "overhead" or "profit," however, even though that is what it is: it is called the sales tax. As such, the sales tax is the Soviet government's most powerful economic tool in influencing consumption, and it is structured as part of the overall economic plan and the pricing policy of the government.

The New Nature of "Sales Tax" and "Profit"

The Soviet Union's use of the sales tax is a powerful tool of economic influence for the government. The sales and income taxes of mixed economies such as those of the United States and Canada are used by their governments to interfere with the functioning of private enterprises. The skimming tax is a tool of the people of the nation, which they can use to control their economy and so bring about economic democracy. Furthermore, the specific character of skimming can be seen only *in combination with the existence of stable prices and the elimination of income and corporate taxes* as they now exist, and so is distinguished even more from the sales tax of both planned and mixed economies. In this regard, as we have said, the existence of stable prices gives the notion of profit a new content; it becomes the reward for efficiency and greater productivity on the part of labor.

As explained, by introducing skimming and eliminating taxation, commodity prices would be reduced by the tax component they are designed to reflect. Consequently, the corporation is left with profit, and because we have established stable prices, any increase in this profit will be due to increased productivity and should not be subject to taxation but to *profit-sharing*. It would be logical that the sharing of profits, as rewards for higher productivity, would also not be subject to the social-share tax but would belong completely to the employee. Their social share is paid through their higher productivity and better performance. In this way, profit-sharing would be a real incentive for a better quality of work —partly for material reasons and partly for moral and ethical ones. We will deal with profit-sharing in more detail in the next chapter.

The New Role for the Consumer

The concept of economic democracy is inherent in both skimming and social-share taxation. Once these practices have been introduced, consumers become well aware of their role in the economic system of which they are a part. If the changes we have proposed are implemented, the advantages for this type of democracy will quickly become apparent. For one thing, consumers will know how much is charged in each dollar for government expenditures. Today, they are not at all aware that all the taxes are projected in consumer prices, and that they have something like 50 percent for accumulated taxes in each dollar spent. This new knowledge, we hope, will induce them to act on and make sure of their democratic right in the election process.

All these changes would, of course, require time-consuming legislative and administrative measures, yet if we are aware of what our goals are, we can make some changes that can take effect immediately. For instance, with regard to profit-sharing, we could abolish or substantially reduce any form of taxation just from the wages increased by profit-sharing. We could lower the taxes on corporate profit for corporations that introduce profit-sharing. We could certainly take social-welfare programs like child care, care for the elderly, and others from the national budget and entrust them to private or charitable organizations or a combination of both. To finance these changes, we would divide the income tax of high income groups into two parts, one to go toward the national budget in the conventional way and the other to go into social-share programs and so toward the care of children and the aged directly. Thus, we could step by step reduce the government's activity and its cumbersome bureaucracy, which according to many estimates very often absorbs half of the allocated budget.

Once we have made the first, however modest, steps, we will be moving in the right direction, and will provoke a growing number of citizens to be involved in such changes and to use their democratic rights to help introduce more and more humanistic aspects to the social life of their nation.

9
Profit-Sharing: The Cornerstone

Profit-sharing is not only the logical conclusion of the analysis of a modern economy but is also an absolute precondition for change. Profit-sharing could mobilize a mass movement to overcome the tremendous inertia in our thinking and acting—particularly the inertia in institutions. On top of that, profit-sharing can be applied to limited goals; it need not wait until we have finished all legislative and other measures necessary to economic reform. We are concerned with immediate action. We want to move today. We shall see that profit-sharing—to a certain extent, at least—can be immediately introduced and become a vehicle for progress, pushing components of our economy further and further toward the desired goals. In this sense, we regard our study as a guide to the proper direction for each step along the way.

Profit-sharing, in our view, will improve not only the relationship between capital and labor but also the working of the whole socioeconomic system. Profit-sharing is first of all to be seen as an ethical principle. We cannot accept—and we have given ample examples—the notion that economics should be value-free and that economic science should be concerned only with the allocation of resources without regard to human values. The ethical principle of profit-sharing lies in the fact that everybody who contributes to the betterment of the nation should be rewarded accordingly. We feel it is not ethical to accept increased rewards without a corresponding increase in one's effort, productivity, and efficiency; but it is equally unethical to accept the benefits of this increased effort without permitting those who bring the benefits about to enjoy a share. We would say that the ethical content of the responsible society is that it accepts the responsibility of giving rewards according to contribution, and demands the responsibility that each individual contribute to the wealth of the nation.

Our social systems have proved to be dehumanizing. The reason is that this principle of responsibility has been voided. The Soviet sort of planning is most dehumanizing, because it insists on target figures that lead to a bureaucratization of the whole economy. It leaves no space for initiative and commitment and responsibility, but orients and limits the minds of workers on all levels to fulfill quotas. Prices and rewards are both centrally planned. Profits are the result not of efficiency but of arbitrarily planned components. Even if the concept of profit is introduced in planned economies, it is not profit in the sense used in a free-enterprise economy—and particularly not in the sense used in the context of the responsible society.

In the more democratic type of socialism—like that, for instance, in Sweden, where political freedom is maintained, and where neither the state nor the leadership of a political party owns the means of production—we see a dangerous development despite the fact that for the time being the material standard of living is still high. We see danger in the erosion of responsibility. "From the cradle to the grave," the citizens are supposed to be cared for by the state. Once welfare is oriented not toward the needy, once its content is not humane charity and care, and once it becomes the principle on which the whole economy operates, it loses its original human character. Parents are not responsible for the welfare of their children; the parents fill out forms and the bureaucracy "takes care." Children have no responsibility toward their parents; forms have to be filled out and the bureaucracy does the rest. When the individual is not responsible for his future, forms and bureaucracy take care. People welcome security, of course, but they pay the price. Their work and their relation to work loses its real meaning. Rewards are guaranteed because one exists; and not because one makes a real contribution to the well-being of the community. Yet it is neither the state nor the government nor the bureaucracy that actually rewards. All the state gives (never mind the tremendous cost of an army of bureaucrats) is part of the prices the consumers pay in taxes—a high, progressive system of taxation that punishes those who contribute the most to the wealth of the nation, and that kills initiative and commitment by eliminating incentives and responsibility.

If a country like Sweden still produces a high standard of living, it is not only because it is rich in natural and per-capita wealth but also because the work ethic is deep-rooted. The decline of worker morale, the frightening degree of suicide and moral decline, and a high rate of inflation are symptoms of a serious malaise to come.

To be sure, the democratic economies, as we painfully notice, have shown signs of strain and failure. We feel this is partly because society has removed or diminished the responsibility on which the system should work. One's original motivation for work is for one's own and the family's survival. Our society is now about to eliminate this motivation. Further, the opportunity for incentives is not widely available to labor today. We don't sufficiently reward labor for better work and increased productivity, and we neglect the worker's incentive for self-improvement. A society based on incentives for the individual to better his or her lot is the society of the future. We therefore look at work incentives as shares in the end result of labor production. If labor were to share in production and be able to retain that share, all these incentives would be there. *This is profit-sharing pure and simple.*

The ethical principle of the Judeo-Christian philosophy —"the laborer is worth his hire"—is expressed in profit-sharing and in the economic theory of a responsible society. This ethical pledge is in itself a sufficient motivation to introduce profit-sharing as a general system. Yet apart from this ethical imperative, profit-sharing is a method without which a mature economy cannot attain full employment and a stable price level.

We have explored the problem of full employment and the tools the government has to use in order to make full employment possible—or, to be more exact, to give everybody who wants to work an opportunity to do so. Still, without profit-sharing, we cannot achieve full employment. Typical for a mature economy, as we have shown in this study, is a dynamism of production. With the same input, we will be able to achieve a higher output owing to better organization, market research, marketing, improved technology, and other factors. We can achieve more production with the same input of wages and salaries. In other words, we will have produced more without increasing the purchasing power.

This means that the sum total of rewards—wages and salaries—would remain the same; and since the increased production would not be matched by increased income and the goods could not be sold, we would have to reduce production. Yet this reduction would lead to a corollary reduction in employment—putting people out of work. In order to stop this unemployment in the past, economists introduced government spending for work that had no economic meaning, and even for "non-working." Such programs lead to an increase of taxes, which in turn leads to an increase in prices (inflation), to an increase of the national debt, with interests to be paid out of taxes, and so on. Yet if we introduce profit-sharing, we can thus match the increased production that is achieved through the higher productivity of labor.

We should further see in unemployment one of the most dehumanizing phenomena of our contemporary economy. Some economic theories justify unemployment. They maintain that unemployment is inevitable, and certain economists are now advocating that 4 percent unemployment should be defined as full employment. This means that hundreds of thousands of unemployed should, "by definition," not be employed. Such an attitude of value-free economics is by far not value-free. It is a theory that justifies crimes against people, depriving them of their basic right to earn their living in a dignified way, and to contribute with their efforts to the well-being of the nation and the family. These theories are free of ethical values but full of non-ethical values. We must fight against such theories. The principle of profit-sharing disproves the theory of the inevitability of unemployment. While we have shown that to fight unemployment we have to introduce a number of measures, particularly government lending, we have to face the fact that these measures cannot guarantee full employment *without profit-sharing.* Yet profit-sharing by itself will not guarantee full employment if it is not accompanied by the measures previously described, such as stable prices and government lending.

It is of primary importance to avoid *inflation,* which deprives the whole economy of its rationality and becomes a disaster for the majority of the people. Inflation deprives the nation of the soundness of its currency; it destroys the value and meaning of well-earned rewards; it attacks the subsistence of people living on fixed incomes, particularly retired people; it affects the whole educational system as well as the system of law enforcement. Still, we are exposed to theories that speak of the inevitability of inflation. The most widely accepted theory is expressed in the so-called Philips curve, demonstrating that a tradeoff between unemployment and inflation is inevitable. Both evils are thus theoretically justified.

In an economy with stable prices, the principle of profit-sharing is actually a necessity. In many countries, price and wage controls have been introduced, and, without exception, have proved to be a failure. A wage freeze is the most uneconomical measure imaginable; so is a profit freeze. Rewards should increase. This increase is an incentive without which no economy will function. Profit-sharing will be a permanent incentive; it will be practically the only increase in rewards. To increase rewards by increasing prices is not profit-sharing in the true sense, because only nominal wages and not real wages will grow. Workers are interested not in how much money they get but in how much they can buy for their money. To get, say, 5 percent more wages to meet a, say, 7 percent inflation means that the worker actually loses. Without stable prices, in other words, the value of profit-sharing will lose its importance. Yet without profit-sharing we cannot maintain stable prices. We have seen that a lack of profit-sharing leads to unemployment, and this in turn leads to inflation. Profit-sharing will thus be instrumental in avoiding both evils.

Profit-sharing has been introduced in many enterprises, primarily at the request of management. It was expected that profit-sharing would increase the interest of the workers in higher productivity, make them more interested in the performance of their enterprises, and help them to feel more a part of the production process. In most cases, these expectations have been fulfilled.

The Application of Profit-sharing

In practice, profit-sharing has taken many forms. In some cases, a fixed percentage of an enterprise's profits has been given to workers, depending on the length of their employment. Rewards for work have been paid in cash, in the form of shares of stock in the corporation, or by a combination of these. At times, such payments are deferred until retirement, and then paid in the form of increased pensions. Some studies have found that profit-sharing has helped a business not just because the employees were getting more but because they felt that the concept expressed a humane approach to their problems and appreciated attempts to create a better working climate and increased understanding between management and labor. The result was better performance.

In the large amount of literature on the subject, many different aspects of profit-sharing have been considered, and attempts have even been made to recommend compulsory profit-sharing on a national level through legislative measures.

Quite a number of views express the expectation that profit-sharing would be the most effective way to fight inflation, since any increase or decrease in wages would result from an increase or decrease in productivity. Some economists have advocated that the market should lower the wages of unskilled or unqualified workers below the minimum wage level, and all labor would then be paid according to its ability to produce. However, in our mind it is doubtful that such measures could ever be implemented; and, even if they were, it is not certain that either inflation or unemployment would be reduced.

In the first place, productivity is only partly due to the skill and effort of the workers. As we have mentioned, the level of technology applied to production, management, research, marketing technique, pricing policies, quality of design, and many other factors that have nothing to do with the quality of labor are decisively of more importance in the success of a business. Although a lack of interest in work, absenteeism, and other labor-related elements can be detrimental to the performance of any enterprise, efficiency and productivity are not solely dependent upon the ability of workers to successfully fulfill their tasks. Poor management, bad design, and other such problems can be the source of poor performance in an enterprise. Consequently, even if wages were stabilized, the danger of inflation caused by inefficiency would not necessarily be eliminated. Furthermore, the market these theories speak about does not actually exist. In a "labor market" containing two highly organized and powerful partners, the role of supply and demand is certainly diminished.

Some authors also assume that profit-sharing would eliminate the conflicts between management and labor. Although this is possible, it is also probable that new conflicts would arise. The question of how large a portion of the profit would be shared would certainly become an issue, and there would also be the problem of how large each individual share would be, coupled with a constant pressure on the part of labor to increase its share of the profit.

Yet such a conflict would be desirable. It would demonstrate the interest of the workers in the profitability of the enterprise. Management would be exposed to a permanent pressure to optimize its performance. Thus even when the pressure of the market weakened, the attempt of the workers to achieve high profits (and a higher share of profits) would be one of the most important incentives in improving the effort of both management and workers.

In our view, this effect of profit-sharing will become increasingly important. In our developed economy, the factors of applied science and mass production have created large corporations. The mere fact that big corporations exist means that they have great power on the market compared to small corporations or consumers. Further changes in big business— whether changes in organization, in policy, in the mode of production, or in the product itself—are far more difficult to bring about than they are in small business enterprises. So big corporations are by their nature less sensitive to impulses from the market, and, consequently, the competitive character of the market becomes imperfect. This is the price we have to pay for the advantages of large-scale production. We cannot have the advantage of mass production and the elasticity of a small workshop.

Still, it would be desirable to reinforce the competition and the intensity of market impulse. The pressure of the employees to achieve higher profits through better performance in order to have higher rewards through profit-sharing would actually be the same kind of pressure a perfect market imposes upon corporations. The pressure to increase productivity, to improve performance, and so to increase the gross national product, would then have two sources—one the market (an imperfect device) and the other the pressure from profit-sharing. These combined forces would become a powerful economic impulse for better performance.

Profit-sharing would stimulate entrepreneurs because they would feel that their ownership would be guaranteed. The workers would be stimulated because they would have a share in the profit, and their efforts would be worth more. The enterprise would be in the hands of responsible entrepreneurs and a responsible labor force. The final results would be available to the labor force just as they are now available to the shareholder. So labor's working effort would be rewarded by corresponding remuneration.

Objections to Profit-Sharing

There are four main objections to profit-sharing. First is that profit-sharing may not be a forceful incentive. Suppose that a corporation makes 10 million dollars' profit, and that the rate of profit-sharing is 50 percent. If this corporation employed, say, 10,000 workers, the share for each employee would be $500 a year—and this increase of rewards would supposedly not be a strong enough incentive.

In answer to this objection, we ask if there exists any real alternative. If we accept the principle that rewards may be increased regardless of increased productivity and efficiency, we must suffer the consequences of inflation. Wages will rise but will inflate prices, and any additional income will be lost to the market. Furthermore, inflation leads to a decline in the quality of life, and also, as we know, to unemployment. A genuine increase in rewards must be based on increased productivity.

In economic reality, there is no other way to increase real wages but by participation in the profit, so long as the profit is the result of high productivity and not the result of price increases or a decrease of quality.

But there is, in our opinion, another more important

point. If we introduce profit-sharing, we expect that the attitude of workers toward their work would change—we could avoid strikes, slowdowns, absenteeism, waste, lack of initiative, and other problems that restrain productivity. The whole system should and would change. The workers would feel not that they were exploited but that they were participating in the result of their efforts.

What we thus introduce is a basic change. In the present system, the means of production and the results of production are owned by the same people. In a system of profit-sharing, the result of production—profit—belongs to both the owner and labor, and so the workers would be most interested in keeping the enterprise healthy and producing. If they simply achieve increased rewards without increased efficiency, a lack of means for investment would soon wipe out the enterprise. But if rewards increase according to increased productivity, we must realistically expect that the profit will grow; it may be doubled or tripled or even quadrupled; consequently, the workers' share will not be negligible.

In order to make this increase of rewards meaningful, we must avoid taking away the increased profit of the corporation. In our system, we have lowered or abolished corporate taxes through the establishment of skimming taxation; we must also make certain that the income from profit-sharing is not diminished by taxes. Thus the objection that profit-sharing would not be attractive may be true under the system that exists now, but profit-sharing would have a different character —and particularly a different scope—in a system that is geared toward profit-sharing and in which profit-sharing is seen not as a managerial gadget but as a basic principle of the economy.

The second objection to profit-sharing claims that if profit is shared losses must also be shared. In our view, wages and salaries are rewards for services delivered. Wages and salaries will not actually increase because of profit-sharing.

They remain the same. Profit-sharing is an *extra income,* a *special premium* for higher productivity expressed in higher profit. We introduced the principle of stable prices. If wages and salaries are stable, real income will be stable as well; and any increase by profit-sharing will increase the *real* income. Under present conditions, this is not guaranteed, for real income is being diminished through inflation. If no profit was achieved, or even if a loss occurred, the nominal and real wages would remain stable. Under such conditions, we would expect that employees and their trade unions would pressure management to increase its efficiency. Employees would thus express their desire to make full use of the potential of the existing capital and introduce the important element of harmony between capital and labor.

The only time we would agree to the workers' sharing losses as well as profits would be if the workers were to elect representatives to sit on the board of directors of a company. The shareholders must take losses if their board of directors is unable to produce profits. If the members of the board of directors are nominated not only by the shareholders but also by employees, then it is logical that shareholders *and* employees must share the responsibility. Unless the workers then shared losses, the representatives of the workers on the board of directors would have rights without being responsible for how they made use of their rights. We would introduce in this way a lack of responsibility into the highest echelon of management and undermine responsibility as the basic principle on which any management must be based. Profit-sharing should not be combined, therefore, with sharing losses. Only workers' participation in management justifies participation in losses.

The third objection is that of the trade unions: that wages and salaries should be uniform in a particular industry. The principle of profit-sharing does not affect this uniformity. As explained, wages and salaries would remain stable, meaning that their present structure could remain stable as well. As a matter of fact, because the rate of inflation is different in many parts of the country, the real wages are not now uniform; only the nominal wages are.

Profit-sharing as explained in this chapter affects only the reward for increased productivity in a particular business enterprise. It is desirable under the system we have proposed that the increase in productivity also be uniform in a particular industry. In order to achieve this, the respective managements must be under pressure to improve their performance. Thus, the uniformity of rewards is to be seen as something to be achieved, and not a mere administrative principle.

The fourth objection deals with the fact that trade unions have achieved a certain power position over a long period of time and would be unwilling to give up some of the power they have acquired. When the principle of profit-sharing is applied, wages might no longer be a topic of trade-union negotiations. Let us suppose that there is a stable price level. Under such conditions, there would be no reason to negotiate an increase in wages. The negotiations for increased wages are now motivated by increased living costs. But if the cost of living did not rise, the space for wage negotiations would actually be very small.

We are speaking of profit-sharing, of course, under the assumption of a stable price level; and we have emphasized that a stable price level is an essential precondition of profit-sharing. Taking this into consideration, we would assume that the scope of protection of union members would even increase. Trade unions would have to be concerned with the stability of prices, and could play a most important role in the organizations dealing with price stability.

Apart from this, an entirely new field of activity and responsibility would come into being. Trade unions would be vitally interested in the performance of the business enterprise and its productivity. The productivity is, to a remarkable degree, dependent on working conditions, and so a greater emphasis on this vital human problem would be a logical consequence of labor participation. As already mentioned, the trade unions would pressure the managements of less-efficient corporations producing fewer profits to improve their performance. This, in turn, would require that the trade unions be equipped with the expertise to make their pressure more effective. This means that the harmony between capital and labor is not identical with the harmony between management and labor. We may envision many conflict situations, but we feel that such conflict is in essence positive, and would lead to better performance in the economy as a whole. The trade union would thus come to protect not only the interests of its members but the economic interest of the nation as well. This would be in great contrast to the present situation, where an increase in wages leads to a price increase, and an unnecessary and basically unnatural conflict between trade unions and consumers in general arises.

Labor unions should be concerned first of all with *real* wages and the increase of *real* wages. Such concern would make the role of labor unions greater, more important, and more effective than it is at present. In the interest of the workers, unions should orient their concern to the optimal performance of management.

Two Questions

We now turn to the essence of the problems of profit-sharing and ask two questions. First, since nothing could be more expressive of economic justice and the interests of both capital and labor than the sharing of rewards by those who helped make them possible, why has profit-sharing not become the focus of a mass movement on the part of labor and its leaders? Second, what role would profit-sharing play in a

150

democratic, human-centered economic system? Is profit-sharing a measure derived simply from the desire for a just system, or is it at the same time a substantial part of the package of measures on which a new, humanistic economy must be based?

A Lack of Incentive for Profit-Sharing

In discussing the Industrial Revolution, we mentioned that the fight for better working conditions and higher rewards, which was the essence of the workers' movement at that time, had a tremendous impact on the application of science to production, and made it possible for wages and profits to grow at the same time. The increase in wages and the standard of living of the working population was due to two factors: first, the impact of modern technology, and second, the relative stability of prices, which were expressed in "money" that had intrinsic value.

We now have a distinctly different economy. We have created a system in which it is possible for the purchasing power of rewards to be stolen by inflation. This is because increased rewards and profits are not under all circumstances the result of higher efficiency and productivity but can also be the result of increased prices.

Under such conditions, the morale of labor is being eroded. Because of the relationship between wages and prices, higher rewards can be gained through strikes and negotiations. Workers have begun to realize that they are no longer rewarded because of their ability and effort but because of the power of their unions. Not only is working morale beginning to disappear but a new type of alienation from work is developing. Furthermore, since wage increases are no longer the result of increased productivity, although labor receives more money, this money is losing its purchasing power. As a result, labor and the rest of the entire nation is facing a decrease of wealth, a decline in the quality of life, and a lack of economic security.

It is our feeling that as long as this type of immorality prevails and the ripoff philosophy on which our economy has come to be based dominates, we face a serious obstacle to the introduction of profit-sharing. The fight for profit-sharing must be paired with the fight for full employment and stable purchasing power in the same way that the fight for these goals must be paired with the fight for profit-sharing.

The Need for a New System

The desire to end inflation and unemployment and to receive wage increases as a reward for contributing to the well-being of the nation could create a new social and political climate in which profit-sharing would be possible.

We repeat that we must be aware of the fact that a *real* increase of rewards is possible *only* under conditions of profit-sharing, and that profit-sharing is meaningful *only* if it is based on *full employment and stable prices*. In addition, we must remember that this is not simply a matter of desire or of declaration but of creating conditions, both in theory and in practice, under which a system supporting profit-sharing can function.

Profit-sharing has not yet succeeded because the lack of morality in the economic system does not permit such a just and moral measure to be applied. This applies also to the group controlling the destiny of the nation—the parliament or the Congress.

Profit-sharing should not remain a managerial gimmick but should be a principle on which a new economic system will be based. The government must take measures to insure that this principle is generally accepted. We don't have in mind any new administrative measures and government interference. Profit-sharing could be made so attractive to both capital and labor that they would voluntarily accept the advantages of this system. Now to the second question.

The Role of Profit-Sharing

The important role of profit-sharing is derived from this new understanding of the economic system. We would like to repeat that profit is to be seen as a most important economic incentive, and our concern has been to create conditions under which there is not only pressure to increase profit but also respect for the moral content of profit. Profit should become a measure of efficiency, and so a measure of the extent to which individual corporations can contribute to the wealth of nations. This can be accomplished only through the introduction of stable prices, which prevent profit from being made simply through price increases.

Furthermore, we have introduced profit-sharing in order to insure that all those who contribute to efficient and productive economic performance should receive a portion of the benefits that accrue from this performance. Such moral values must be introduced into the working of our economic system.

The Humanistic Revolution

The application of a humanistic orientation to our socioeconomic system does not involve anything closely resembling a social or economic revolution. It requires a new frame of reference for economics, new concepts, new theories, and, most important of all, *a revolution in thinking. A revolution of the mind could and should bring about a new evolution of the society.*

Furthermore, we feel that a most realistic approach to our goal is through an appeal to common sense. If this approach fails, the prevailing philosophy of bread and circuses threatens us with the same future as that of the Roman Empire.

The Economic Impact of Profit-Sharing

Having emphasized the moral and ethical impact of profit-sharing, we turn now to the second question: the economic impact of profit-sharing in a mature, human-centered economy.

It is typical of a mature economy that innovations of some importance have become difficult. Even developing a new type of automobile takes many years and costs hundreds of millions of dollars. It seems that the more advanced science becomes, the more costly further research is; and the risks in developing and applying new methods, technologies, designs, and innovations also increase. In addition, research for the civilian sector of the developed countries is low, especially when compared with research and development expenditures for military and space programs.

This unfortunate situation is compounded by the fact that large corporations are not under much pressure to make use of their potential to introduce innovations, while labor is either not interested in or is even opposed to innovations, out of fear that it could harm employment or rewards. It is therefore necessary to introduce a *new* form of economic pressure. *Profit-sharing could and should become such a pressure on management.* Labor's interest in increased profits will thus be channeled to an interest in introducing innovation, and will force enterprises to introduce innovations in areas of both production and management. This, in turn, will increase not only the standard of living of labor but of the nation as a whole.

Organizations of both manual and mental workers would be more interested in investigating all possibilities for increased production and in applying those techniques which

154

prove effective. Under the present system, where initiative of this sort goes unrewarded, there is no incentive for unions and their members to support such efforts.

In spite of this, we cannot expect an ideal situation. Profit-sharing will certainly result in a more demanding labor force. But while conflicts over wage increases are now usually solved at the consumer's expense, the new system will limit the effects of solutions to the realm of the individual enterprise. As a consequence, labor unions will be in a position to protect their members *as consumers* while defending their members' interests as workers. This will further increase the nation's respect for the unions, since they will have the interests of all consumers in mind.

If we introduce profit-sharing based on full employment and a stable price level, we can assume that it will have a tremendous impact on the Soviet bloc. While unemployment and inflation constitute a powerful propaganda tool for the Communist countries, our new system could trigger a demand by labor for a share in the profit that would reward each worker according to his contribution, and so become a powerful force to improve the dismal conditions in that part of the world.

Harmony Between Capital and Labor

We particularly welcome the idea that profit-sharing can create a harmony between capital and labor—this being one of the most important imperatives of social and political harmony. In order to make our position clear, we would like to summarize what kind of harmony we foresee, and also what we understand the concept of capital and labor to be.

Our concept of harmony between capital and labor is based on ethical values—values that the Judeo-Christian philosophy developed. We have tried, therefore, to project these values not only into the behavior of individual economic actors but in economic theory and the practice of economic systems as well.

Because "capital" has become a household word and is interpreted in many ways, we would like to make clear what we understand it to mean. In a mature economy—which is a gigantic transformer of natural forces and wealth into productive forces and the wealth of nations—capital is the material part of the transformer, and labor the human part.

Capital has more forms than its monetary one. We believe that capital is the result of the effort of practically the whole working population of a nation, and of many generations. Even if a growing proportion of the working population is active outside the factories, their activity is still an integral part of the gigantic transformer; and the capital used in research institutes, laboratories, transportation, banking, in the education systems, and elsewhere matches capital—money—as a means of immediate production.

Yet capital is meaningless without the human part of the transformer. It is *created* and *used* by human beings. Although the technological side of capital is the consequence of applied science, it is not in itself the source of wealth, however important it may be. Initiative, commitment, working morale, skill, expertise, working conditions, human relations, meaningfulness of work, space for self-realization—all these and many related factors are of crucial importance.

Only if we create harmony between capital and labor will we be able to mobilize these factors. Such harmony is not brought about by administrative or organizational measures. Nor can it be created simply on the level of individual enterprises. What must be achieved is the creation of forces that foster harmony. We have to deal with such factors as human nature and many conflict situations and conflicting interests that are due to human nature.

We are particularly concerned with measures that will affect the economy as a whole. Therefore, we will have to see the importance of creating measures that allow work to benefit not only the individual but also the nation as a whole. We hope to create a social and intellectual climate that will have a harmonious impact on individual workers.

If we have a system of trade-offs between inflation and unemployment, we create a climate not of harmony but of fear, uncertainty, and disunity. If we have a system that permits and justifies increased rewards without increased contribution, we create a lack of responsibility and conditions in which disharmony will flourish. It is stable prices, a just redistribution of income by the skimming tax system, profit-sharing, and other measures that will contribute to the spirit of harmony in the society.

While profit-sharing by its nature is a measure that will be applied to business enterprises, it should be seen primarily as a measure of importance to the whole social fabric and an important component in humanizing the economy and harmonizing human relationships. In our concept of capital and labor, we do not see harmony as a kind of "detente" or an appeasement of foes. We see in labor and capital an integrated, organic unit, and find that the existing disharmony has been created by neglecting the ethical content of the Judeo-Christian philosophy in building our mature economy.

Our present economy imposes on us too great an influence from a philosophy that interprets the relationship between capital and labor as inherently antagonistic, with the advantage of one to be bought at the disadvantage of the other. This view not only explains the relationship of capital and labor in terms of antagonism but *creates* and even propagates antagonism.

Capital and Ownership

It is a natural part of the democratic system that many forms of ownership coexist. Individuals, shareholders, coop-

157

erative forms of ownership, workers themselves may associate to create business enterprises. Communities may have their own corporations. The only reservation we have in this respect is against state ownership. Although there may be some cases, such as a central bank or some similar institution, where state ownership is preferable, in principle we feel that the government has to be an organ and servant of the nation and not an entrepreneur or an owner of capital.

The more enlightened critics of capitalism, who do not attack the form of ownership alone, oppose it because of the great concentration of economic power, which implies political power. Yet the power of large corporations, and the possibility that this power will be misused, lies not with the size of capital but with the lack of economic democracy that could channel the effort of all big or small corporations toward goals that would be binding on both government and corporations. The principle of *profit*-sharing should also be one of *power*-sharing. All measures we have advocated logically lead to a *just share of profit* and a *democratic share of power*.

Our concern is *whom* the economy serves. We will judge an economy by the degree to which it respects human values, to what degree it offers human freedom both in the realm of politics and economy, to what degree it is concerned with the harmony of human relations, and, in particular, to what extent it is based on the harmony of capital and labor.

We see profit-sharing as the decisive instrument to achieve this harmony, and we have explained that in order to make use of this instrument a nation has to apply a series of measures. By this system, labor and capital can become complete partners in production, and thus in the profitability of the company. Workers would supervise themselves— there being no need for "capitalist bosses" when workers have a personal stake in their own work. At the same time, the shareholders would demand that management develop the best skills and methods to enhance production.

The result would be more goods of higher quality at lower costs, and more and better services that were less expensive. Young people would not have to worry about what to expect after they complete their education. Our freedom would be enhanced, because government would not inhibit production. We could become a model for the rest of the world.

If equitable profit-sharing systems were operating in our industries, we would not have the labor-capital confrontations that are plaguing us. We would not have the wage demands we are experiencing; and no government intervention would be required in contract negotiations. We would be nearing the closest labor-capital accord that has existed since the beginning of the Industrial Revolution.

We have tried to show that we have within us the means to control our fate. We offer not a detailed blueprint but an orientation—a chart. It could and should be a starting point to move toward a brighter future. We owe it to ourselves and to generations to come.

A Lack of Human Values

One of the wisest thoughts of the Judeo-Christian philosophy has been forgotten—that *man does not live by bread alone.* This philosophy recognizes the necessity of bread, the material side of life, and hence the importance of the development of technology. However, we do not live on bread alone, and the consequence of our forgetting this may one day be a society where even bread is not available.

In both the West and the East, we are confronted with a technocratic approach that assumes science and technology will solve all of our problems. The technocrats offer us bread, and this is good; but they ask us to pay for it with our humanity. The target figures of the Eastern technocrats and the rate of profit of those of the West may differ in some respects, but they have the same philosophical roots. Under their system, human beings are reduced to objects in any economy of planning and profit; there is no room for the human dimension in these systems or in their philosophies. Aside from the different rhetoric and private language in which their theories are formulated, the "economics" of the East and the West are frighteningly similar in their anti-God and antihumanist attitudes and philosophies.

We are facing a renaissance of Marxism. Although in different forms and often in different concepts, and in spite of the criticism directed against its application in Socialist countries, Marxist philosophy is beginning to have a new impact in Europe as well as in the nations of the Third World. This same trend can be seen in the United States and Canada, although at a slower pace. And what is most phenomenal about this trend is that Marxism appeals to so many people, despite the fact that wherever it has been applied it has not lived up to a single claim of Marx or any of his followers.

The supposed goal of the Marxist philosophy, the establishment of a humanistic society where all people are respected and ample opportunity is offered for fulfillment, self-identification, and self-realization, has been achieved in no Marxist society, not even to the degree that it has been achieved in the so-called capitalist societies. This aside, the important question is, Why has Marxism, despite its tragic failures, become the dominant world view of our age?

The Appeal of Marxist Philosophy

The conventional explanation that most people are not aware how difficult life is in a Marxist system is too simplistic. A great deal is known about the oppression and the low standard of living under this system; and even among those who live in socialist countries, are dissatisfied, and are active dissidents—despite the tremendous risks—all too many are opposed to the alternative system of capitalism.

The appeal of Marxism lies in its pretended concern for real human problems. It is a philosophy that claims the establishment of a humanistic society. It is not sufficient to prove that Marxism leads to the opposite of what it claims. We must be able to offer a workable, humane alternative to the Marxist approach—an alternative that has a truly humanistic society as its goal. If we accept our own system, with its unemployment, inflation, and technocracy, we fail to check the appeal of Marxism to all those dissatisfied with such a system.

We should orient our own system toward the dignity and majesty of human beings. If our opposition to Marxism boils down to an opposition to a *particular* form of ownership, and objection to *certain* shortcomings, or to a disagreement with *certain* principles in Marxist societies, then we are nothing more than critics. But if our opposition is dictated by a truly humane concern and genuine objections to a dehumanizing system, then we must begin to combat the dehumanizing elements of our own system and provide a workable alternative.

A System of Thinking Human Beings

The philosophers of capitalism perceived the economy in terms of the division of labor; the invisible hand and economic laws such as the supply-and-demand relationship were the decisive forces in determining the motion of the economy; profit was the highest economic value. Marx regarded the economy as part of a natural historical process; he saw the history of man as a history of class struggle that was determined by eternal laws. Capitalist economists see a system of commodity relationships in the economy; Marxists see a system governed by laws. Our perception of the economy departs radically from both of these views.

In economic terms, we realize the importance of material incentives, but we emphasize the fact that human values must have a dominant position; we accept economic growth as an important concept, but we focus on the structure of the gross national product and the orientation of the society; we support science and its application, through technology, as one of the foundations of a successful and efficient economic system, but we stress the importance of regarding science and technology not as ends in themselves but as the means by which we can fulfill humane responsibilities.

We regard a socioeconomic system as a system of thinking human beings. Further, our achievements, whether they are beneficial or detrimental to man, are our responsibility, not governed by abstract laws. In perceiving the economy in this way, we are attempting to develop an alternative to Marxist models as well as to the Western technocratic model.

We repeat again and again that profit-sharing must be seen in this wider context. The philosophy from which profit-sharing is derived must be a philosophy applied to all aspects of the performance of the economy. Bearing this in mind, we would like to repeat that profit-sharing is a tool that can be introduced and used immediately. We could and should act now.

Profit-Sharing: Let's Start Tomorrow

The concept of profit-sharing can be introduced immediately. We need not wait until all the conditions discussed in preceding chapters are met. Even if profit-sharing were realized on a small scale, it could immediately bring remarkable benefits.

We assume that the government could make use of its

162

tool of taxation. It could decide that when an employer agrees with the employees to share the profit on, say, a 50-percent basis, the employees could pay no taxes, or only minimal taxes, on the income that is the reward for higher productivity. They would pay normal income taxes only on their regular wages and salaries. They could receive their profit share either quarterly or at the end of the year. The profit would be figured on the basis of net profit—after taxation. We think it realistic to expect that the introduction of such measures would have manifold effects.

First, it would express the appreciation of the government for increased productivity; and by not taxing the rewards for higher productivity, the government, as well as the employer, would grant a benefit. We would then expect that the workers would put pressure on management to be as efficient as possible. They would compare the scope of profit-sharing with other business enterprises and insist that their share be at least as high as that of similar enterprises. In this respect, they would have parallel interests with the shareholders, and would create some elements of harmony between capital and labor.

Since the share of worker profit would be based on the business's after-tax profit, the workers would soon realize that their share was made smaller by corporate taxes. They would feel in their paycheck that they were helping to meet government expenditures; and they would be interested in joining all those who object to unnecessary government spending. In this respect, also, we would find a parallel interest between capital and labor. Now corporate taxes per worker per year in both the United States and Canada represent nearly $1,000.

We could go one step further and suggest that the employees use their reward from profit-sharing to invest in business enterprises that have high priority for the economy of their country. Then the profit from this income would not be taxed at all. We would thus find an additional income and incentive for profit-sharing. For instance, if one buys, from his profit-share income, certain shares which pay a 5 percent dividend, and this income were not taxed, it would channel remarkable sums into badly needed new industries. Particular advantages should be given when the rewards from profit-shares are invested to support industries of the workers' own country, or when workers buy up shares of foreign-owned corporations.

These measures would certainly increase the interest of tens of thousands of workers in the economic performance of the economy, and would be of great educational value. Apart from the workers having a growing interest in seeing the government spend only where it is absolutely necessary, the fact that in this and other instances labor will find itself on the same side of the barricade as capital will bring a quick understanding of the essential meaning of our concept of harmony between capital and labor. This practical education is important in clearing away the current confusion in the workers' minds. They are taught that government is the institution that pays the bills, where in fact it is the workers, directly and indirectly as workers and consumers, who are paying all the bills for the government expenditures. Thus, profit-sharing would end up as one of the important counterbalances, and the system of balances and counterbalances would be greatly strengthened. Finally, we assume that once such measures have been taken by the government, it will not be necessary to use or misuse the power of the government to force employers and employees to agree on profit-sharing.

We have emphasized that profit-sharing must be established on a national level. Yet this does not mean that it has to be forced upon the economic actors. In our view, the proposed profit-sharing would be so attractive to both capital and (particularly) labor that this attractiveness could bring about profit-sharing on a national scale. The principle that labor is not to be taxed and punished for improved performance is in itself both just and economically justified and attractive, and must have a tremendous appeal to all citizens. The adoption of profit-sharing would also be a practical example of how government should act in the economic realm. We do not need regulations and interference with business enterprise, nor a new governmental body with added bureaucracy, to implement profit-sharing or other new elements. Government should make rational use of the existing tools, such as taxation, and leave the rest to the economic actors. They will find their own interests and act accordingly.

The issue is not, as it is often stated, between no state interference at all and all the power to the government. The government is supposed to be the servant of the nation; and we must distinguish exactly where its services are needed and where they are detrimental. We need profit-sharing to become a system in which the action of the government is applied to the whole economy. There would be two ways to do this.

One way would be to ask the government to make laws, to enforce profit-sharing, to determine the conditions of profit-sharing agreements, to create a profit-sharing agency on federal and provincial or state levels, to employ an army of bureaucrats, to use profit-sharing for political purposes.

The alternative—which is the way we have chosen—is to create certain conditions that make profit-sharing attractive to labor, to capital, to employers, to trade unions, and to the nation as a whole. Then it is up to those involved to find—even by trial and error—the best forms and ways to implement it. We expect that once this method has been introduced and found to work, the role of government will be discussed and treated on a new plane. We will have to be ingenious and find such ways that will involve the least government interference.

Adam Smith spoke of the invisible hand that would harmonize the many different economic actions based on contradictory interests. We need a *visible* hand. Yet this visible hand should be that not of a spiritless bureaucracy but of a sensitive government that would create conditions to channel the actions of *free* labor and *free* enterprise toward the interests of a *free* nation. If any of these three freedoms is offended, the visible hand will not be that of a serving government but of a dictatorship.

The introduction of profit-sharing will also demonstrate that it is possible to introduce incentives that meet the needs of both labor and capital; that there is no either-or; that there are both. It will show that it is both possible and realistic to believe that we can create incentives that are oriented toward the benefit of the nation and toward all who contribute to its well-being. But—and this is the most important lesson—we will succeed only if we base all economic considerations on humane values, on a just appreciation of everybody's attempt to improve their contribution to the good of themselves and their community.

10

Capitalism or Socialism: Are They the Only Alternatives?

Having explained an economic system based on the Judeo-Christian philosophy, we now think it necessary to consider some of the alternatives. First, we will deal with the alternative of capitalism or communism and ask to what extent these systems are related to the Judeo-Christian philosophy. We also feel it important to consider two rather new phenomena, one dealing with the idea of workers' participation in management (which many people see as a panacea) and the other dealing with the role of the multinational corporations, which on the one hand are criticized as being among the greatest evils of our days, and on the other hand, are praised as the first steps toward an integrated new world order.

The Emergence of Capital

Because of the Industrial Revolution and the division of labor, there has come into existence a growing number of employees, more and more machinery, a greater supply of raw material, more buildings and industries, and a general increase in commodities related to the production process. Another name for these commodities is capital, and the owner of the means of production is called the capitalist.

Usually we speak also of capital as meaning money, credit lines, shares of stock, bonds, and so on. We call these items capital because they are components of the economic process that creates profits and interest. We could call these items "liquid capital" as opposed to "producing capital." Even Marx, who was everything but an admirer of capitalism, wrote in his *Communist Manifesto* that the capitalist class had achieved greater progress than any other class in history; at the same time, of course, he blamed the capitalists for making the lives of the workers miserable. It is certainly obvious that both "liquid" and "producing" capital are necessary to make full use of the potential offered by the division of labor and the new modes of production. Still, we think that Marx did not grasp the essence of the concept of capital: *Capital is a transformer of natural forces and natural wealth that makes output greater than input.* The Industrial Revolution created such transformers as steam engines owing to the contribution of the organizer, the inventor and the entrepreneur. The essence of capital is not that it is owned or in what form it is owned but that it is the *result of a higher level of thinking and creativity.*

In any consideration of the capitalist system, however, it is important to realize that control of the means of production and the so-called exploitation of the working class is typical not only of capitalism but of any system wishing to achieve industrialization. The industrialization of the Soviet Union, for example, required far greater sacrifices from the workers than that of England or any other capitalist country. In addition, these sacrifices are justified by the theories of both systems: Adam Smith placed the responsibility on the invisible hand, and his followers developed this concept into economic laws; Marx's followers utilized laws of "socialist accumulation" to the same end. A simple example will illustrate this point. As long as farmers have no technology, they will work endless hours at strenuous labor. If they hire laborers, those laborers will also have to work hard. The farmer will earn little, the laborer even less. When modern technology is used, the hard labor will be done by tractors and combines. Shorter working hours, less physical strain, and higher earnings will follow. It does not matter whether the farm belongs to an individual or is a Soviet collective farm. What matters is what technology is used and how efficiently. In other words, on what intellectual level the productive process is based.

Finally, once this initial period of industrialization has passed, and the application of science to the production process follows, such an increase in the output of goods and services will occur that the acquisition of capital and increased rewards for work can go hand in hand. This is possible because of an additional economic revolution—that in science and technology.

Revolutionary Change in the Essence of Capital

In viewing development as a product of the level of thinking applied to production, we find the existence of two distinct types of capital. The first is that of an economy based on the level of thinking which produced the Industrial Revolution. This revolution created a new social structure composed of a class of owners of the means of production—the capitalists—and a class of manual laborers. Because this economy was based on a relatively low productivity of labor (compared with that of today's economy), the accumulation of capital was closely tied to low rewards for the working class: Profit and low wages were in a way interdependent.

The second type of capital is that which developed out of the Scientific-Technological Revolution. During this period, the application of a higher level of thinking, that of science, to the means of production changed the production process, and hence the very essence of capital in a revolutionary way: it permitted the growth of capital and profit in conjunction with a growth of income for the working population. To be more exact, as the economy was based increasingly on a higher level of thinking, the standard of living for workers rose, and they consequently spent more. This growth in worker income became one of the preconditions for the growth of the economy as a whole and for the production of profit and capital.

Today, in spite of the existence of fewer manual workers and a reduction in working hours and working effort, we are still able to produce far more goods of better quality than ever before, including many goods that could not be produced in more primitive economies.

In considering the efficiency of capital, we find not only that it has increased tremendously but also that it requires the entire system to work as a whole rather than simply exploiting one component of it. In order to maintain peak efficiency and keep production high, we must continue to apply science, make full use of effective management techniques, and, most important, keep in mind the needs of the consumer. We must keep all the components of our economy running smoothly to realize our fantastic potential for capital.

In spite of all that we have said concerning this new type of capital and its tremendous impact on our socio-economic system, most of us still conceive of capital and capitalism in terms of the economy at the time of the Industrial Revolution. We are inclined to see only the formal side of ownership rather than "capital" as an integral part of a perfectly new society. If we compare the societies of America or Western Europe today with those of the 18th century, we quickly realize that, despite similarities in the form of ownership, a brand new form of capital has emerged— automobile factories, machine-tool factories, television, telephone, radio factories. Perhaps 90 percent of what factories now produce did not exist in the 18th century.

Two Basic Questions

To free our minds from outdated concepts concerning capital and the form of ownership, there are two basic questions that can be asked in reference to any socioeconomic system. The first question is whether this system is based upon experience gained from the working process, upon inventions characteristic of the Industrial Revolution, and consequently, primarily upon manual labor. If the answer is yes, we have an underdeveloped economy—an economy basically different from the developed ones, an economy where consequently all concepts have a different meaning compared with corresponding concepts of our economy. Or is it typical of this system that science is being applied to production and that the role of manual labor is declining while that of brainwork is increasing? If this is so, we have a developed economy, a new economic system, and must derive all our economic concepts from this new economy. In this respect, both the nations of the West and Japan and the Soviet Union and its satellites in Eastern Europe would merit an affirmative answer to the second question.

A further question is whether any of these countries has created a system where the population has its proper share of the created wealth of the nation, and whether the people have the right to determine how this wealth should be distributed.

Today, capitalism typically exists within the framework of political democracy. In spite of this, the right of the people to decide economic questions is limited. In fact, faced with inflation, unemployment, and a general decline in the system as a whole, even the most powerful labor organizations are as helpless as their governments seem to be. These countries are missing that part of a fully functioning economy which would be sensitive enough to the responsible will of the people to bring about a change in the orientation of the system and redirect it toward full employment, stable currency, and an increase in the quality of life.

Political and Economic Democracy

The notion that the form of ownership determines our economic life has been so ingrained in us under capitalism and communism that it will be difficult to do away with. Yet it is important to remember that the form of ownership is only one of many dimensions determining the structure of society.

In contrasting the two concepts, we can see that the democratic system in which capitalist economies operate provides relative freedom for the task of expanding political democracy to the economic realm. The challenge is to formulate the complex measures that must be introduced to achieve this goal, and it is through this book that we hope to meet this challenge. Conversely, the communist countries are void of political democracy. As long as the citizens are deprived of this basic human right, there will be no chance for economic democracy to develop. The last attempt to establish a democracy within the framework of socialism, to build "socialism with a human face," as it was called, was in Czechoslovakia in 1968; the movement ended with the Soviet military occupation of the country.

In the democratic capitalist world, such an attempt to create a society "with a human face" has up until now not been made, even though the necessary freedom exists. For this we are critical of this society; we are more critical still of communism, for it does not permit people even to discuss the social system, let alone attempt to humanize it.

Socialism as the Absolute Form of Capitalism

If we accept the notion that capitalism is a system based on meeting the interest of the owners of the means of production, then the Soviet model would in a sense be the most capitalist system in the world. In that system, the owners of the means of production would be the Communist Party leaders, for they have absolute command over the production components of the economy. No trade union, no parliament, not one other institution or group has any voice in the production process. Thus, the system has lost its balances and counterbalances, and has developed into an absolute form of capitalism, respecting only the interests—whatever they may be—of the actual owners of the means of production. In practice, the interests to be satisfied are those of the Politburo. The motivation of power far exceeds any profit motivation. Consequently, the police, the army, the Party, and the government apparatus get the overwhelming share of what is produced, while the people as a whole are kept at subsistence level.

We run into difficulty in interpreting capitalism from this angle. Actually, we would do better to speak in terms of a concentration of power or control: To be exact, we could say that Soviet communism is based on the absolute monopoly of capital by a single group, while in capitalist countries we find a diversity of owners of the means of production.

The point is that a concern for the traditional concepts of capitalism and socialism is both misleading and, as the military wars and cold wars of this century have shown, even dangerous. We should be concerned not with mere ownership but with profounder questions. What is the role of humanity in each system? Does the system benefit the entire nation or only a few groups or individuals? What are the goals of the system, and, if they are just, what means are being used to achieve them?

One way in which traditional economic concepts can confuse us is in our contemplation of certain socialist countries. Sweden and Norway, for instance, maintain political democracy, and a private ownership exists there. Yet while we do appreciate the remarkable degree of democracy in those countries, we cannot overlook their movement toward the Soviet model. The trade unions are beginning to concentrate so much economic and political power in their hands that they are coming more and more to resemble the Communist Parties that have concentrated *all* power in their hands. The Soviet Union achieved this stage by revolution, of course; our fear is that other countries might achieve the same result by evolution.

At the time of the Industrial Revolution, when production was not yet based on applied science and its decisive element was that of manual labor, the ownership of the means of production *was* the outstanding characteristic of the economy. One of the most important sources of capital was savings:

People had to save in order to accumulate money or goods for obtaining capital, and many people were forced to "save" to this end. This "forced saving" was carried out by paying low rewards—subsistence wages—to the workers; it was in this type of saving that profit was made. Marx called this form of profit surplus value—the difference between the value of what a worker produced and the amount of money he was paid. In this type of economy, it was primarily the owner of the means of production who reaped all the benefits of ownership; the workers earned only what was necessary to keep them working.

All this changed when science was applied to the production process, and these changes can be demonstrated by means of a simple example. Let us compare a watermill that produced power to run machines in the economy of the Industrial Revolution with a water-driven turbine used in today's electric-power plants.

The Importance of WHAT Is Owned

The owner of the watermill was the one who benefited most from this method of transforming the natural force of moving water into a productive force that could be used to power machines in a factory. Because this new form of energy was cheaper and more efficient than manual labor, it could replace many workers and increase its owner's profits and its capital. Regarding the humane orientation of the watermill economy, we could focus on the owner of the watermill and ask the owner to sacrifice profits and share benefits with others by charging lower prices or by increasing the wages of the workers; we could even suggest that if the watermill was owned by the workers themselves, the benefits of this new form of energy would be more equally distributed.

On the other hand, the type of watermill resulting from the application of science to production is something completely different. We no longer have a watermill but instead a hydroelectric plant. It may still be privately owned, but is it the same capital? Can we ask the same questions as those addressed to the owner of the old watermill? To clarify our point, let us consider some additional differences between the socioeconomic systems of the past and those based on applied science.

The Social Benefit

First of all, there is a great difference in the amount of social benefit derived from the application of science to the production process. For instance, the electricity produced by a hydroelectric plant appears in endless forms in practically all households and businesses, and not just in a single factory. In fact, this energy became an essential part of the society. Electric lights, radio, television, medical and other equipment —millions of goods and services have been produced and used with the help of this electric power. By imagining what life would be like without electric power (or by simply remembering the consequences of the most recent power failure), we can easily understand that the "gain," or social benefit, that results from the transformation of natural forces through applied science spreads throughout the whole of society and affects the quality of life of the whole nation.

Certainly, new and different questions must be formulated for this system. For instance, it will be of great importance to determine how this electrical energy is to be used. For war or for peace? For the benefit of society or for its undoing? Will everyone be able to make use of this energy? Will the dam of the power plant create some ecological damage with irreversible consequences for ourselves and our environment? Will the production and use of this energy contribute to inflation or to unemployment or will it be used in ways that stimulate the economy?

176

Second, the owner of this plant will be able to increase the wages of the workers and, at the same time, increase the profits. Consequently, the main source of profit will not be in low wages or high prices or in "saving"; instead, it will be based on the effectiveness of the plant. Thus, profit depends on the level of applied science, the ability of the designers of the plant, and its management, on the development of the hundreds of thousands of factories and goods and services that make use of its electricity, on the way the income is distributed, and on monetary and fiscal policy. In effect, profit depends on the efficient functioning of the entire socio-economic system.

The Humane Avenue

The owner of the plant should be guided by ethical principles, of course, and keep in mind the questions we have raised, but the awareness and actions of individuals can hardly affect the performance of the economy as a whole, and perhaps not even of the owner's plant. What becomes of primary importance in a system of this type is to bring about changes in values and attitudes that will have an impact on the working of the entire system. The problem is how to project the humanistic values of the Judeo-Christian philosophy not only into the realm of our ethical behavior but also into the economic system.

With this in mind, it should be clear that to regard capital merely in terms of the form of ownership and not as a transformer of natural wealth and forces into productive forces and wealth for humankind is misleading. Our concern must now be to create a system in which the potential benefit from applied science can be realized and increased, while at the same time being oriented toward the benefit of all people responsibly involved in the economy.

The Cooperation of Capital and Labor

Further, we must realize that our "transformers" are initially only potential "transformers" and that our interest must not be in this potential in itself but in the way our "transformers" are able to make this potential a reality. As long as we have plants and factories that do not realize their potential, they are plants and factories only in name. A plant that does not operate or that operates at a loss is worthless; it is costly, it benefits no one, and it may even be harmful to our socioeconomic system.

The more efficiently a plant functions, the more energy or goods will be produced at lower cost, and the greater will be its benefit to the nation. This increased efficiency is not simply the result of existing "capital," of a plant itself, or simply of "labor," but of a meaningful cooperation between the two. Both are components of one transformer of natural wealth, and both are essential to increased efficiency and must function as a single unit in order to produce it. It is our feeling that one of the best methods for insuring that this cooperation takes place is through the creation of a system that is conducive to such cooperation.

The form of ownership in any system varies in its importance, but it is not the decisive factor. There are a number of decisive factors. One is *what* is owned (a horse-driven cart or a computer); on what level of thinking this "capital" is produced and managed (a factory run by a watermill or a factory run on atomic energy); whether there is a spirit of cooperation between worker and owner; and, finally, upon what values the economic system is built and toward whose interest it is oriented. These must become our essential considerations.

178

Either-Or?

In practice, we are confronted by two economic systems. One is based on the philosophy developed by Smith and Ricardo, the founders of capitalism, and the other on that by Marx and Engels, the founders of communism; both of these philosophies are from a past age. We now turn to the question of which of these two systems is best suited to realizing our desire to reorient the economy toward the interests of human beings, and, in doing so, to achieve and maintain economic stability involving full employment, stable prices, and ecological equilibrium.

There are those who feel that it might be possible to combine the advantage of both systems and create a new economic philosophy and system on that basis. Others feel that such a synthesis would not be possible, and that the question is basically one of either-or. Let us take a brief look at each of these economic systems as they exist today and find the answer for ourselves.

The Self-Adjusting Forces

The classic philosophy of capitalism posits the existence of self-adjusting forces in the economy. Through these forces, free enterprises, while pursuing their own interests, would follow economic laws of nature and create a state of economic equilibrium involving full employment and stable purchasing power. Government interference in the economy should therefore be nonexistent or kept to an absolute minimum.

During the nineteen-thirties, it became obvious that this self-adjusting ability of the economy was lacking; the Great Depression was proof of this. Nevertheless, the concepts of laissez-faire capitalism and the invisible hand were not so easily relinquished. John Maynard Keynes theoretically justified the existence of economic self-adjustment *and* its limitations, and, at the same time, developed an economic theory that asked for government interference through methods such as government spending.

The free-enterprise system and a competitive economy brought about a most natural development—that of the dominance of stronger economic components over weaker ones. The conflict on the market between large corporations and small business enterprises on the one hand and between corporations and consumers on the other created a situation in which large corporations or corporate groups dominated the market and often eliminated competition altogether. In this situation, relatively powerless consumers found themselves in a market controlled by the producers, and their right to choice of products, while not eliminated, as in planned economies, was severely restricted. The economy had become geared to the interests of the powerful components rather than to those of the consumer and was, as such, *business-oriented* rather than *consumer-oriented*.

The Road to "Overgoverning"

The economic, social, and political implications of this development induced the government to interfere with the economy. Increasing government interference naturally creates a cumbersome bureaucracy, which, in turn, contributes to the existing imperfections in the economy and the market. Yet the absence of government interference could lead to a complete breakdown of the socioeconomic system.

Owing to the structure of political democracy, political decisions and considerations began to influence the methods of government interference in the economy and, step by step, to limit the freedom of corporations. In this way, economic and social demands made on the government have forced it to become the greatest component of our economy, absorbing about a third of the gross national product every year.

From Limited Freedom to No Freedom

The large, powerful domestic corporations that exist in almost every nation of the world are typical of a mature economy. Similarly, multinational corporations are typical components of the world economy; they developed as the most logical and effective form for national corporations operating on an international market to take. If the immense power of these corporations undermines the principles of free enterprise, then obviously we must develop the means through which free enterprise can be promoted in spite of it. In other words, we should find a way to establish a competitive market in an economy which requires that corporations be large and powerful to function efficiently, and particularly a way to give the consumer the right to choose. We understand free enterprise to mean the freedom of the producer as well as the freedom of the consumer. The economy is, after all, production for consumption. These two components are like two poles of a magnet. There cannot be a magnet with one pole only, nor should there be an economy with the freedom of only one of the two components.

Regardless of what *should* happen, what has actually happened is that we have begun to fight one kind of concentration of power with an even greater concentration of power, to fight the lack of free enterprise by eliminating it completely through government intervention.

The assumption that a bureaucracy would be more concerned or more efficient in dealing with the proper functioning of business enterprises than the present system is in absolute contradiction to all experience with bureaucracy. The great task, as we have said, is to reduce the tremendous power of the government. Rather than expand the scope of government interference in the economy, we must limit government activity in those areas over which business enterprises have control.

It is important to realize that a system that fosters inflation, unemployment, a lack of concern for the natural environment, and a disregard for human needs creates a socioeconomic environment that puts pressure on its participants to act in the same antihuman direction. All this orients the performance of the economic system against the basic interests of the people. It is consequently misleading if we put the blame on individual businesses for succumbing to the pressure of the government. In fact, if we do this, we let the government, the defendant, play the role of the plaintiff. If we have an economy in which it is possible, and even theoretically justified, to have, for instance, rewards (profit, wages, and salaries) increase without a comparable increase in the productivity of labor and the efficiency of production, we must blame the system, not its components, for the inflationary tendencies that will be produced; the system's corporations and businesses are simply acting according to the rules of the game as witnessed in Canada and the United States and the rest of the Western world in recent years.

The only effective solution to our economic problems is to develop a philosophical base for our economy that will make the economic system work toward the interests of the nation as a whole. As a result, the components of this system will be under pressure to operate in the same manner. Such a solution is complex and will require sophisticated measures.

Meaningful Free Enterprise

Free enterprise cannot be interpreted merely as the freedom of business enterprises to do whatever they wish. The concept of free enterprise must also include the freedom of the consumer to have his needs met, the freedom of the worker to be rewarded according to his contribution to the increased wealth, to the "plus" that is produced, and the freedom of the nation to decide the orientation of its economy and the goals this economy shall attempt to achieve. To correct the shortcomings of the present system by giving the government the freedom to make arbitrary decisions concerning the economy, to concentrate all power, and to deprive people of their basic democratic rights is certainly not a good alternative to the economic evils we may wish to eliminate.

Under our present system, the government already has too much power and control over the functioning of the economy. Already, the government's fiscal and monetary policies limit freedom at the level of the individual enterprise to such an extent that the government has an impact on every decision made by a business or a corporation. A greater awareness of the fact that—because of administrative, monetary, and fiscal measures—enterprises are unable to realize their fantastic wealth-creating potential would force us to rethink the government's role in our economic system. Changes must be made that will *cause the government to become the servant rather than the master of the economy* through economic democracy.

The Marxist Alternative

As we have pointed out, the founders of capitalism and their followers, the contemporary economists, assume a self-adjusting capacity of the economy. Some of them feel that some help is needed and that the government should interfere to make the self-adjusting forces more effective. Marx actually accepted the notion of a self-adjusting capacity of an economy that is based on private ownership of the means of production. Yet he claimed that these self-adjusting forces always function to the benefit of the owners and are detrimental to the workers, the actual creators of wealth. According to Marxist philosophy, the economy will serve the workers only when the means of production were taken from the hands of private individuals and returned to their "rightful owners," the working people.

Absolute Freedom at the Enterprise Level

In practice, this philosophy justified the expropriation of the means of production and led to their appropriation by the government. In Marxist countries, of course, where the government is actually under the control of the Communist Party, it has been Party leadership, as "representatives" of the working people, that has gained absolute economic control and has all attributes of an owner. In a tragic sense, absolute freedom of the owners of the means of production had been achieved. The entire economy became one single enterprise, and its manager, the Politburo, possessed absolute freedom of action; interference through competing enterprises, consumer or political rights, or from the marketplace, had been eliminated.

In the same way that an individual corporation must plan its activities, so also the activities of the sole national enterprise of the Marxist model must be planned. The entire economy is broken down into target figures for production. Creative thinking is permitted only in the central planning body of the country; all the other participants in the economy may think only in terms of the target figures assigned to them. Human beings become as much an object of the economic plan as any commodity in the system. Furthermore, by underestimating the importance of human creative ability and eliminating it from the economy except at the very highest level, this system has created a most inefficient economy. In addition, it is an economy in which its consumers, its citizens, have no rights and no say.

In summary, we might say that a free-enterprise system that is truly free is possible only in a democratic society, and that a democratic society is possible only under conditions of free enterprise. We cannot overemphasize the importance of the concept of freedom of enterprise, so often misused and misinterpreted, and its many meanings. In the context of this book, it means the freedom of management; the freedom of workers; a responsible partnership between labor and capital; and the freedom of the consumer. Freedom of enterprise consequently means a free marketplace in which competition exerts pressure on business to be efficient and sensitive to the rights of consumers. It implies that the economic system is not overgoverned, and that the government will act only in areas that cannot be dealt with by individual enterprises or groups of enterprises—such areas as government lending, the structure of the skimming and social-share taxes and foreign-trade agreements. And finally, it means the freedom and duty of trade unions to protect their members both in their capacity as producers and as consumers. Free enterprise is being portrayed as an evil force operating to the detriment of our people and their economy. As a matter of fact, the problem is that the freedom of enterprises is being violated. The government's interference, its misuse of scarce capital resources for wasteful and unproductive projects, is one of the primary causes of our problems. The nonproducing sector of our society grows. Fewer citizens are left to bear an increasing tax burden, productivity falls, and there is less national wealth to share. Unemployment is being created and pseudo-welfare measures that contribute to the inflation are introduced, thus depriving the truly needy of their social benefits.

Government must serve the people, not the people the government and its overlapping and costly bureaucracy. The history of the United States and Canada gives ample evidence that it was free enterprise that made these countries wealthy. This freedom is now endangered.

11

Two New Phenomena: Worker Participation and the Multinationals

The Birth of Worker Participation in Management

At the end of World War II, the attempt to overcome the deep moral, political, and economic crisis of Europe brought new elements in the labor movement to the political scene. In Western Europe, particularly in France and Italy, strong Communist Parties emerged and contributed to a general radicalization of the labor movement. Even in countries such as West Germany, where the communist influence was negligible, workers demanded more participation in management.

Generally speaking, there are three separate forms of worker participation: The first is based on the application of Marxism and the nationalized ownership of the means of production, and has been introduced in Yugoslavia. The second is based on a democratic constitution; ownership is primarily private, although the nationalization of a portion of the means of production plays an important role, like Western Germany, France, and other countries. The third is in preparation in Sweden.

Worker Participation in Yugoslavia

Yugoslavia's economy was at first based on the Soviet model: the strict planning of, and absolute control over, the economy, as well as all other facets of economic life, was in the hands of the Communist Party. However, conflict between Yugoslavia and the Soviet Union developed because the Soviet Union insisted that it had the right to interfere with the sovereignty of all socialist countries. Having fought so bravely for their independence, and having paid a heavy price in their fight against the Nazis, the Yugoslavs were not prepared to give up their sovereignty, and consequently parted with the Soviet Union.

In order to extricate themselves from a most difficult political and economic situation, the Yugoslavs turned to the

West for economic aid, and switched their economy from that of central planning to a market economy. Since the ownership of the means of production was already nationalized, the Yugoslavs introduced a new concept, according to which the workers were regarded as the *economic owners* of the business enterprises in which they worked.

While many different theories of ownership exist in Yugoslavia, the principle is that the nation is the *legal owner* of the means of production, while the workers are the economic owners. The workers take the profits as well as the losses from the enterprise, but they do not have the right to dispose of the enterprise; only the legal owner—the commune, or the local government has this right.

Apart from agriculture, of which over 90 percent is in private hands, and small business and handicraft enterprises employing no more than five people, all business enterprises are "owned" by the communes but controlled by the workers. The workers elect a Workers' Council, whose function is to decide matters of production, investment, and financing, how the "gain" will be distributed, and how to make decisions concerning the principal issues of business and organization. The Workers' Council elects the members of the Executive Committee, which is responsible for implementing the policy of the Workers' Council. The director of the enterprise is also elected by the workers, who choose one of three candidates nominated by the Workers' Council. In practice, particularly in the bigger enterprises, the director and his or her staff make the major decisions, for complicated questions of investment and business policy can be decided only on the basis of expertise and cannot be entrusted to majority vote by those who lack sufficient knowledge.

The rights of the workers are limited by the influence of the leadership of the Communist Party. Although the party does not interfere directly, it has the final say on who will be candidates for the directorship. Since all power is concentrated in the party leadership, and hardly anyone dares to go against the party, even a small hint of policy has the effect of an order. Further limitations are imposed by the local governments, the communes, who take the role of the trustee of the enterprise and who are responsible for its losses. The communes are strongly influenced by the party apparatus and are used to impose the party line upon the enterprises.

The influence of the banking system in Yugoslavia upon enterprises is extremely great. First, there is the impact of, as the Yugoslavs call it, the "bank of all banks" in the banking system—the National Bank. Owing to the fact that there is no money market, the National Bank is solely responsible for the money supply. It also decides how great the reserves of the commercial banks will be, and determines the rate of interest. In these respects, there is little difference between the National Bank of Yugoslavia and the central banking systems of capitalist countries. With regard to the commercial banking system, however, Yugoslav commercial banks represent a great concentration of economic power. Seventeen of the largest banks in Yugoslavia represent 94 percent of the entire banking potential, and, accordingly, have tremendous economic power and large profits.

Although the capitalist types of owners of the means of production have been eliminated in this system, the Workers' Council and the workers act in the same manner as the board of directors and shareholders of any capitalist enterprise would. They are concerned with the profit of the enterprise and the share of the profit, with no regard to the needs of the economy or of consumers' rights. On top of that, the larger enterprises have tremendous political power, because the great number of workers employed in each enterprise enables them to push their interest or the interest of their enterprise above that of the consumers, the market, or the needs of the economy as a whole. They will consequently put all their weight behind an increase in price for their own products and behind getting their own rewards, with no regard to productivity.

As a consequence, a very high rate of inflation exists in Yugoslavia at the present time. The costs of production increased by roughly 100 percent between 1958 and 1972, and the reward for the employees rose approximately the same amount. Yet the price index of consumer goods increased nearly 350 percent during the same period. This means that the profits of the enterprise and the workers far exceeded the actual costs of production. These profits stem simply from asking the consumer to pay far higher prices than are justified by the costs of production—a kind of exploitation of the consumers of which the workers themselves are a part. In addition to inflation, there are half a million unemployed people in Yugoslavia, and a million more have been forced to seek work in capitalist countries such as Germany. Had they not left the country, Yugoslavia would have far more than 10 percent of its working population unemployed.

Rewards in this system are based on a very low minimum wage plus profit-sharing. If the loss of the enterprise is so great that even the minimum wages cannot be paid, the community in which the enterprise is located must make up the difference. Consequently, the citizens of the community must pay for the enterprise's loss.

Despite these shortcomings, Yugoslavia has a more efficient economy than the Stalinist model of the Soviet Union and her satellite countries. Furthermore, the workers and other citizens of Yugoslavia have more political rights than their Soviet neighbors, though definitely less than those of capitalist countries. Because of this, the Yugoslav model is rather attractive to the people in Eastern Europe and in the Soviet Union, particularly because Yugoslavia is a sovereign country that gives its workers the right to codetermine the conditions in their work place, for example.

Nevertheless, the problem of ethnic divisiveness is an

old and unsolved one in this country; further, unemployment and inflation have not been solved. Owing to the absolute concentration of power in the party leadership, the relative freedom—relative compared to the Soviet system—is actually a privilege given by the party leadership that can be unilaterally withdrawn at any time.

Shortcomings of the Yugoslav Model

The shortcomings of the Yugoslav model are obvious. First, instead of focusing on the interest of consumers and giving them decisive economic rights—economic democracy— it is assumed that if the workers in production are given rights within the enterprise, economic democracy has been established. It is characteristic of the Yugoslav model that the interests of the minority in the enterprise dominate the interests of the general consumer, and consequently of the people. Although in some cases the workers may feel that they have a greater say as far as the enterprise is concerned, they still live in a system that is oriented toward the interests of the enterprise rather than toward human beings.

For the time being, a growing tendency toward centralized economic planning and a restoration of the Soviet model presents a permanent danger for both the Yugoslav economy and for the country. While Yugoslav workers have gained a remarkable degree of participation in the operation of their enterprises, because all workers are interested only in improving the earnings of their own factories, all that they have gained as workers they are losing as consumers. For instance, the workers in a shoe factory may get higher rewards. Once they buy the shoes, they will pay higher prices. But as the workers in furniture, clothing, linen, glass factories get the same higher rewards and thus increase the prices, they will often pay more as consumers than they have gained as workers. Apart from this, the workers represent only one faction of

192

the people, and so the people, as consumers, will be exploited by this system.

Worker Participation in Western Europe

The second form of worker participation, applied in Western Europe, also represents simply a reform rather than a basic change. It reforms the so-called capitalist system by offering workers a certain degree of participation in controlling the performance of the enterprise.

Since the end of World War II, although the primary concern of labor has continued to be higher wages, broader fringe benefits and so on, worker participation has become more and more of a central issue on the political side of the labor movement. Demands that labor should be permitted a larger role in the decision-making process of business enterprises have increased in intensity and impact. In Germany, for instance, the Workers Constitution Act was legislated into law in 1952. Under this act, labor has the right to elect a third of a firm's supervisory board, and in the steel and coal-mining industries, a 50-50 representation on the supervisory board has been established. In Holland, Norway, Sweden, and France, similar legislative measures have been enacted, and the United States and Canada may follow suit. We shall soon be hearing new voices in management, from the shop floor all the way up to the board room.

Generally speaking, two forms of worker participation have begun to appear in Europe.* The first takes the form of a labor council or a joint advisory committee composed of both labor and management, which acts in a consultative capacity at plant and company levels. These committees serve

---

* The information contained in this and the following sections is primarily based on an excellent survey of top-level executives in 50 countries from "Worker Participation," by John M. Roach, Conference Board Report No. 594.

primarily as channels of communication, and cooperate with management on nonwage issues; sometimes, the committees deal with specific programs such as welfare, shop programming, and shop planning. This type of participation is being used by management to involve labor in decisions concerning working conditions and other issues.

In some cases, profit-sharing is being considered as a component of worker participation, and the specific terms of its inception are being negotiated as part of labor contracts. Management is usually interested in introducing profit-sharing in order to increase the interest of the workers in profit, rather than in management decisions.

In Australia, labor is represented on a national wage and price commission and various other national bodies. In this case, there are again two types of participation, one at the enterprise level and the other considering wage-and-price aspects of the economic process as a whole.

The second form of worker participation in Western Europe is that which occurs at the level of the board of directors. As mentioned above, worker participation at the board level has been granted in certain cases through legislation in Germany. The Norwegian Labor Party is responsible for legislation that requires companies with more than 200 employees to institute a Board of Representatives composed of one-third employees and two-thirds stockholders.

In the Netherlands, legislation gives workers an equal voice with stockholders and management in the selection of members of corporate boards of supervisory directors. The Danish Social Democratic government has introduced "economic democracy" by establishing a mutual fund of shares in Danish companies, and workers are becoming owners of these shares and so are able to elect board representatives.

The consensus of economists in these countries seems to be that as long as worker participation is related to basic problems and management retains the authority to make final decisions, worker participation is fruitful. More controversial, however, is the pressure to expand worker participation to include long-term decisions or any decisions usually relegated to management or the board of directors.

Worker Participation in Sweden

A major step in this direction has been made through the Swedes' proposed widening of worker participation. Specifically, this move involves a proposal by the Swedish government and the Confederation of Trade Unions of Sweden, according to which the trade unions would control practically any decision traditionally reserved for employers. This would include the appointment of directors and foremen and management decisions involving expansion, merger, pricing, and investment. Further, it includes the right of unions to have full information about a given company's affairs.

The fact that this is a joint proposal by the government and the trade unions attests to the tremendous power of the unions in the economy; this will certainly be the decisive organizing force behind this new form of worker participation. Since 90 percent of the blue-collar workers in Sweden are organized, the trade unions, representing 1.8 million members, will represent both an economic and a political power that will not be matched by any other institution, including the parliament. (In the meantime, a conservative government has replaced the Social Democratic one. It is possible, although not likely, that these tendencies will be reversed.)

The Limited Nature of "Industrial Democracy"

"Industrial democracy," as the system is being called in Sweden, by no means approaches our concept of economic democracy.

Worker participation with regard to basic problems,

to working conditions, and also to a proper communication between management and labor deserves all possible support. Management science is advocating this type of participation, and close cooperation between management and labor is recommended even in countries where such participation has not yet been demanded by labor organizations or the workers. The challenge for management science to adapt the organization of the enterprise to human needs has been derived from practical experience. Management science understands any factory as a human system, and attempts to project human dimensions into the management of systems.

Worker participation in questions and problems that are, by their very nature, managerial problems is, however, something completely different. First of all, such problems require a measure of expertise and experience, as well as a sense of responsibility. A management staff that lacks these qualities should not be permitted to run an enterprise, and, in fact, this is usually the case. But under Sweden's system of industrial democracy, workers participating in management have neither the experience nor the expertise; worse still, they would be permitted to continue running an enterprise even if their decisions proved to be detrimental.

Moreover, labor's decisions regarding management will be based not only on limited experience but also on a desire to do what is best for labor.

In practice, worker participation involves the participation of the workers' organization—the Confederation of Trade Unions, which, like any organization, tends to be institutionalized and headed by a bureaucratic apparatus. Once an organization has many members and great power, the power relationship between the members of that organization and the apparatus of the organization shifts toward the leadership. The situation will be similar to that of the role of the Communist Parties with regard to workers in the Soviet model. The party nominates workers who are members to any positions that are available; these nominees enjoy the power of the party, work toward the party's goals, and are dependent on the party apparatus.

Once the trade unions have the power to control industry, and even to have an influence on hiring and firing practices, they will cease to be the trade unions they were. They will be so in name and by law, but they will cease to be organs of labor and to be dependent on their members; in fact, they will have power over their members. Instead of being an opposing voice to the power of management through which their members can be heard, they may become part of management and will, together with management, be in charge of the workers.

Even if all the democratic rules could be maintained, the role of the trade unions would be changed by a perfectly different climate characterized by a tremendous concentration of power. What is called workers' participation and industrial democracy would actually be the participation of the trade union—of an institution. Because the power of this institution is extremely great relative to the individual members, and because the members are becoming very much dependent on the trade union, a most important democratic component will be missing. Thus, what appears to be a formal increase in the scope of worker participation would actually diminish the active participation of labor in management and replace it with an apparatus belonging to the trade unions, which would run the whole industry.

Once this type of worker participation is applied, we may expect two possible alternatives: On the one hand, the trade-union management will act in a manner typical of conventional management, and the workers themselves would notice little difference. Management would maintain its interest in achieving the best possible profit, and labor would have no organization of its own to combat this orientation. In this case, labor would be worse off than before. We assume that this is the most logical and likely development.

If, on the other hand, the trade-union participation was more worker-oriented than the management, it might attempt to meet the workers' demands. Consequently, management would have to yield to the pressure of the trade-union representatives in the management for increased wages without increased effort, which should normally be resisted by management. If higher wages were permitted without increased productivity, the workers would be acting against their own interests, for as consumers they would lose their rewards in an inflationary market.

Economic Democracy

All our objections thus far have been based on more pragmatic concerns. Our primary objection to the Swedish concept of worker participation stems primarily from its effects upon economic democracy. As we have said, the Swedish trade unions represent 1.8 million members, in a population of 20 million. Actually, the Swedish practice of worker participation threatens the nation with an economic dictatorship of a minority, and a dictatorship not only by labor but also by the trade unions that would control labor. The basic principle of democracy is thus violated.

Our point of departure has been economic democracy based on the orientation of the economy toward the economic rights of consumers. We must create a system in which the consumers—the people as a whole—have the right to decide about the orientation of the economy, and how to make the economy serve mankind.

Economic democracy expresses the right and the possibility of the nation as a whole to determine the most important features of the economy by means of democratic elections.

The factories as the transformers of natural wealth into

the wealth of nations are the result of the effort of the whole working population, and of previous generations. Consequently, we have been concerned with such components as stable prices, full employment, ecological practices, and non-renewable resources. These are the concerns of the whole nation and of future generations.

The interests of individual factories, whether they are owned by one individual or hundreds of thousands of shareholders or the workers employed there, are not identical with the enumerated interests of the nation. We do not achieve economic democracy if workers instead of shareholders have the right to inflate prices, pollute the air and water, waste scarce raw materials and energy. In the last analysis, it would not serve the workers in their capacity as consumers—as consumers either of commodities or of their natural environment. From this angle, we see workers' participation in management and the concept of industrial democracy as missing the problems we are faced with.

Yet from a humanitarian and an economic point of view, worker participation that is oriented toward making work more meaningful, respecting human dignity, appealing to an interest in work, and combating any form of alienation is to be supported. The interest of the workers in the enterprise will be motivated by their knowledge of the problems of their workshop, their ability to participate in decisions about their working conditions, and their right to be informed about the profits in which they share. This sharing in profits is meaningful only when it is based on stable prices. Neither the Yugoslav use of profit-sharing nor its use as a mere managerial gadget is identical with our concept of profit-sharing, where it would be the only way to increase rewards and still be based on stable prices and higher productivity.

It is in labor's best interests to have the most efficient management possible. If the workers in a specific branch observed that in one factory the profit, and consequently the shared reward, was higher than in their own, they could justifiably put pressure on management to achieve the same results. This type of pressure would be, as we have said, a necessary and economically progressive form of pressure, and would foster increased production through more efficiency throughout the economy; with the same input, a greater benefit would reach the entire nation.

Thus, we regard worker participation on managerial questions as pseudo-democratic and economically detrimental. Such practices will not change the basic ills of our society; it is more likely that those ills will be reinforced. Political and economic power will be concentrated in management, and the nation's ability to apply democracy to the economy for its own benefit will be denied.

The Multinationals

We have already pointed out that the division of labor was the first step in the development of the Industrial Revolution. The organizer divided the production process into its simplest components, each worker had only one small part in the production of a commodity, and this division increased the productivity of labor. Further development led to an integration of labor. Commodities became the result of the integrated effort of workers in many branches, of designers, researchers, scientists, of educational, banking, transportation systems, and so on.

The same process can be observed on an international scale. A growing number of products are the result of the integrated efforts of many countries. Although the process of integration between nations is so far not as developed as the domestic economies of highly developed countries, this process in which products are not any longer the result of the labor of one single nation but of many nations became typical of contemporary production. It is in this context that the multinationals should be understood.

The application of science that led to an integration of the working process on the national scene eventually brought about the existence of the multinationals, who apply science, know-how, and entrepreneurship in a number of countries and integrate the manual and mental labor of many nations. Some militant critics of the multinationals—overlooking the fact that the emergence of these corporations is a logical and necessary step in the application of science and technology on a worldwide scale—actually fight not multinationals but the process of spreading progressive modes of production. While attacking certain undesirable practices of the multinationals, these critics do not see that these corporations contribute to the growth of the economy on a world scale. Like the Luddites, who were about to destroy machinery because it destroyed jobs, so would the opponents of the multinationals destroy the pioneers of a new stage of development because of some misuse.

The rise of the multinationals represents an organizational revolution of tremendous scope. The rate of growth of multinational corporations is two to three times that of most developed industrial countries. Multinationals are actually global corporations that internationalize human society. Peter Drucker calls them "global shopping centers." These global corporations plan their activities on a world scale. Overseas factories and other enterprises are not just attached to the parent company but are seen as part of an organically integrated worldwide unit transcending by far the conventional view of national states. For instance, the Canadian-based global corporation Massey Ferguson takes transmissions made in France, axles produced in Mexico, and engines manufactured in Britain and assembles them in a Detroit plant whose output is intended for Canada.

The same internationalization is applied to financing. The Orion Bank, for instance, is organized by Chase Manhattan, National Westminster (U.K.), The Royal Bank of Canada, the Westdeutsche Landesbank Girozentrale, Credito Italiano, and Nikko Securities of Japan.

Avid supporters of the idea of multinational corporations even assume and advocate that the existence of multinationals means the end of national states; and they also envision a kind of global government. We doubt that such a development is likely—at least not in the near future. National states are not mere economic units. They are based on cultural traditions, customs, and behavior. The concept of the melting pot has proved rather fallacious even on a small scale, and would be hard to realize on a world scale. While different cultures will continue to co-exist (and from a humane perspective this would be most desirable), still the international cooperation and integration brought about by the multinationals will have a tremendous and, in our view, positive effect for our future.

The industrialization of England in the 18th and 19th centuries as well as the later industrialization of the Soviet Union, was—as we have already pointed out—connected with great sacrifices by the working population in order that the necessary capital for further growth could be accumulated. The same applies to the underdeveloped nations. They have to pay an even greater price for their industrialization—one that requires far more capital now than in the past. Foreign aid, although it was a help, still contributed very little to the industrialization of the less-developed countries. The great asset of multinationals is not only the capital at their disposal but, first of all, their know-how and their organizational and managerial skills—in other words, the very high intellectual level on which their performance is based. Consequently, the multinationals achieved their industrialization with less pain than was the case in the West or the Soviet Union.

We see, therefore, in the multinational enterprise a vehicle for progress—an institution that is the natural development of the high-level stage of economic performance typical of the leading economies of the world. In this sense, the multinational enterprise is instrumental in the efficient, sensible, and sound development of the world.

What matters today is not the walls, not the machines, not the physical installations; these can be nationalized. But the intangibles—the management, the research, the technology and the access to capital—that are the absolute preconditions of progress cannot be nationalized. They move in the free area of human endeavor, and definitely do not lend themselves to expropriation. In our opinion, this was well demonstrated by Germany and Japan after World War II. Both countries lost most of the material elements that made them great before the war. They were completely destroyed. Yet today, 30 years later, both have overtaken other nations that came out of the war in a much better position, because both countries have developed the intangible elements; they have invented, created, exploited.

During those same postwar years, Russia was speaking out against capitalism as the greatest evil in the world. As a matter of fact, Soviet leaders discouraged developing countries from cooperating with free-enterprise companies. That same Russia, because it is unable to develop management, research, and other such things essential for growth, is now looking to corporations, the great monsters of the capitalist structure, to come finance, build and structure its own business.

Today, the demand to nationalize multinational industries as a response to increased agitation about foreign investment, although a typical reaction of many countries, is contradictory to the development for which they strive and on which they depend.

A nationalized firm could conceivably get hold of current technology, but in a comparatively short time that firm would be hopelessly out of date in its technology, having been cut off from the flow of creative stimuli from the parent company of the multinational corporation. Given a framework of free trade in the world, however, a multinational corporation with its capital, inventiveness, technology, and management skills developed elsewhere, can move them to any country.

In many countries, the proponents of nationalization of multinational industries are becoming more and more militant. Such tendencies can lead only to regression. Any nation committing such expropriation would be closing the frontiers to scientific development made elsewhere. Indeed, expropriation is tempting because it spares the effort of creation, and appears to offer an easy political answer to some economic problems. In the last analysis, it is detrimental to economic progress because it undercuts innovation, which for the modern corporation is a major source of revenue.

Multinational corporations, because of their high level of technology and management, have a domino influence on less efficient businesses, forcing them to improve or be replaced. The Michelin tire plant in Nova Scotia, for example, is forcing the rest of the Canadian tire industry to produce a safer tire to stay competitive.

We have a world with much wealth and much poverty. We want to bridge this gap. Technology and management can bring about more equal distribution of knowledge and wealth. Traditional approaches to achieving this goal through various foreign-aid programs have failed first because political strings that are always attached to foreign aid have a way of diverting or paralyzing economic enterprises, and second because these aid programs are insufficiently concerned with helping a nation increase the level of knowledge necessary for management and production.

Foreign investment by multinational corporations increases the wealth and part of it spreads throughout the economy and raises the general standard of living. A deliberate policy restricting investments by multinational corporations may bring two dangers.

The first would be that instead of importing capital that would produce commodities, the import of commodities would become necessary. This leads necessarily to a loss of jobs. To avoid this, it would become necessary to restrict imports, and it is to be expected that other nations will do the same. Thus foreign trade would decrease and so would exports. Given such conditions, underdevelopment will hardly be eliminated.

Second is the danger that foreign firms, harassed by restrictions and threats of nationalization, would simply depart, as they have repeatedly done.

We believe that multinational enterprises, working on one side for a profit and on the other side supplying capital, technology and management, are more competent than any government agency to cope with development and change in the world. Properly structured, they are collectively the vehicle that can distribute technology and wealth throughout the world on a balanced basis. These are the good aspects of multinational corporations: but what about the negative side?

The first objection critics have is that the multinational corporation is often directed from another nation. They claim that the headquarters does not understand the needs and the problems of the country where its subsidiaries are operating. American companies are particularly vulnerable to this charge. The average United States multinational company derives 80 percent of its income from the American market. In consequence, the weight of total company planning is distinctly biased to the American problems. What is needed for multinational corporations is a set of internationally worked out rules regarding their operations.

A second criticism is that multinational companies have the power to supply sales contracts from any one of their worldwide network of plants. A subsidiary could negotiate a sale and, by head office decree, lose the right to supply the contract. This does happen sometimes, and it is wrong. As long as the subsidiary is profitable in itself, the multinational parent has no justifiable reason for interfering in its operations. Ground rules are needed to stop this.

A third problem with multinational companies—and one of the tragic consequences of the political instability of the underdeveloped world—is that multinational companies are now investing relatively more in the developed countries than in the less-developed countries, where the risk of loss is appreciably higher. There is political instability, with no international protection, for a multinational firm's investments.

We must help to develop the Third World. The multinational way could do it. But, as we have pointed out, the irresponsibility of multinational corporations on the parent level often precipitates political opposition. The reason is that the subsidiary management does not always deal with problems in the best interests of the nation a particular plant is operating in. If subsidiaries of multinational corporations cannot advance because of restrictions imposed by the parent, these restrictions must be eliminated. We should be able to devise a method where one division can handle local problems without destroying the effectiveness of the corporation and its approach to our own development.

We would suggest, then:

- That multinational corporations operate within the correct framework of neutrality, with a majority of its decision-makers on the local level being citizens of the country where the subsidiary operates;
- That future multinational enterprises be set up on neutral ground—with the parent to assist with capital, technology, and managerial skill but never stifling the local development of its subsidiaries;
- That the seeming absolutism of central control (which is, at present, the greatest irritant) be eliminated;

- That major powers of the free world convene an international conference to establish guidelines for the behavior of a multinational corporation in any country. This conference would negotiate treaties covering conditions to be met for opening, running, and closing an operation, for tax treatment, and for transfer prices between stages of manufacture;
- That a permanent international commission be set up to enforce these guidelines, with the appointment and authority of commission members established in such a way as to free them from short-term political influence;
- That each major power *cancel* all foreign aid. Instead, each should commit, on a five-year basis, say, 1 percent of its G.N.P. to a special fund. This fund should be used to back the enterprises in countries that want to help themselves. The fund would be controlled by the commission in cooperation with the World Bank, and no political strings would be attached;
- That nation-states, and possibly specified areas within nation-states, be rated every five years by the commission to determine the security of investments within the country and the degree of development the country needs; and
- That all money invested by the commission be spent in joint venture with multinational corporations, with political risk carried by the commission, and with other risk handled on a normal, free-enterprise basis by the corporation; that is, the commission would insure the corporation against confiscation or expropriation, provided that the corporation had complied with all guidelines. Otherwise, the joint-venture partners would incur the same business risk of profit and loss as any other venture.
- The money put in by the commission should be on a debt basis; the equity should be held by both the corporation and the entrepreneurs of the developing countries.

Therefore, we might approach the problem at a different level—not by nationalizing local subsidiaries but by truly internationalizing the parents. The essence of this suggestion is that world corporations would become quite literally citizens of the world. What this implies is the establishment, by treaty, of an International Companies Law administered by a supranational, nonpolitical body. This body would include representatives from various countries, who not only would exercise normal domiciliary supervision but also would enforce such regulations as an antimonopoly law and guarantees with regard to uncompensated expropriation.

While these suggested measures could eliminate the negative impacts of multinationals, we must be aware that we have social and economic systems that produce unemployment, inflation, and pollution; that destroy human relations; and that disregard humane dimensions. As long as such systems prevail, mere legislative measures to regulate multinational corporations will not prevent these corporations from bearing the marks of a sick society. We should be aware that this malaise is not inherent in the multinational corporations but is a manifestation of the malfunctions of our economic system.

We should therefore not see in the problems of multinationals a problem independent of the properties of the economic system. We must build first of all an economy based on the human-centered values of the Judeo-Christian philosophy, with all the balances and counterbalances necessary for economic stability and growth, and for the betterment of people, and thus create conditions in which the great potential of the multinationals can be fulfilled.

12

Conclusion: Toward a Responsible Society

Today, we live in one of the most sophisticated societies that man has ever been able to devise. We have reached greater heights of intelligence, and attained more knowledge than at any previous time in our history. We would like to believe that ours is the greatest civilization that has ever been known. Yet we live in constant fear, constant anxiety, constant turmoil. Why is it that man, with all the experience and knowledge he has acquired through the centuries, is unable to produce a society that eliminates these negative forces? *Why do they seem to be increasing rather than diminishing?*

In the past sixty years, we have seen communism emerge from a meager beginning to a force that threatens to destroy the free world. And in that same period we have seen the democratic form of government move from constructive, humanistic approaches for solving humankind's problems to becoming defensive and apologetic. Our concern is where all this will lead our civilization, and how long this state of affairs will continue.

Why don't we eliminate poverty when our economy has the potential to provide for more than the needs of all its citizens? Why are more resources spent for the development of atomic energy for war than for peace? Why do we spend more on research for the space program than on programs dealing with health and the quality of life? Why do we have inflation when growing technology could make all goods and services less expensive? Why must we be threatened by the possibility of a war in which both sides would be destroyed? Why is technology used *against* man instead of for his benefit?

No one wants war, unemployment, inflation, pollution, poverty, or the decline of our civilization, yet who can we blame for the fact that all of these exist? It seems that we have lost the ability to control our world. It appears that an invisible, intangible, and powerful force—the force of our own technological age—has control.

In this study, we have tried to demonstrate that such invisible forces do not exist in reality, and have tried to give an answer to the great and tragic "WHY?" We have tried to demonstrate that the mortal dangers we face are neither inevitable nor the consequence of some anonymous force. It is "we," ourselves, who are responsible for all these evils; and, consequently, we are the ones who have the ability to change our society and adapt it to our needs.

We have also attempted to show an avenue that would lead us toward humane goals, being fully aware that the methods we have devised bear the limitations of the human mind. We expect and hope that others may find better and more adequate solutions; and we would be happy to support them. This, however, is not the crucial point.

The crucial point is found in our assumption that society must be seen as a system of thinking human beings — that we human beings are the creators of our society and can shape its future. We must become aware of our responsibility for creating a RESPONSIBLE SOCIETY. The RESPONSIBLE SOCIETY will have to help every individual produce what is maximally possible. All people, in every organization and in every institution, will be stimulated to do their utmost to improve their own lot and their own social and natural environment. Such a society can demonstrate that all the evils we face are inherent neither in history nor in human nature. These are the basic assumptions on which a humanistic society must be built.

These basic assumptions are deeply rooted in the Judeo-Christian philosophy of humanity. Although we may adhere to the ethics of this philosophy individually, its tenets have not been incorporated into our social, political, and economic system. We have created a *spiritual vacuum* and allowed it to be filled with antihuman concepts. We have forgotten the role of human beings as a subject of history, and have perceived them only as its object. We have not been duly concerned with creating an anthropocentric society—one in which human beings are the measure of all values. Instead, we think in terms of profit, power, number, classes, and races. Human beings have been reduced to cogs in the social machinery.

However tragic this situation may be, the lesson we can draw from it is extremely encouraging. It shows that once we underestimate the role of humans and their spiritual and emotional capabilities, no achievement of human creative genius can save us. Neither the most fantastic technology, nor material wealth, nor the mastery of natural forces will serve humankind in the end. In fact, all these may contribute to the final undoing of humankind. Overall, we have found that our civilization cannot survive unless we succeed in building a society, and particularly an economy, on the values of the Judeo-Christian philosophy—the values of the total, responsible, creative human being.

Our desire and aim has been to demonstrate that such attempts are possible, and that from this point of departure we may arrive at new conclusions and concepts, even in such remote areas as monetary, fiscal, and taxation policy.

We hope that our approach will contribute to the awareness that such great changes in the orientation of our society are possible, and that this may trigger all people of goodwill to control their own future and that of coming generations. In this way, they will create a political climate and forces strong enough to mold history.

We would like to repeat with the greatest emphasis that this book is not to be seen as a blueprint, or, for that matter, as the revealing of absolute truth. We regard it as a challenge to others to discuss our views, to improve where we have failed or made mistakes, to be critical and show further ways to accomplish the great task of building a humane and RESPONSIBLE SOCIETY.

A Note
About
the Authors

STEPHEN ROMAN was born in Velky Ruskov, Slovakia, in 1921. After attending agricultural college in Kosice, he left Czechoslovakia at the age of 16 and emigrated to Canada, where he worked as a farm laborer in Port Perry, Ontario, and then on an assembly line in Oshawa. During World War II, he served in the Canadian Army, and, after the war ended, he began to build his business. In 1945, he organized a mining group that successfully developed oil and gas interests in Western Canada and the Williston Basin of North Dakota. In the early 1950s, he disposed of his interest in this syndicate to acquire the property at Elliot Lake, Ontario, which he developed into the world's largest uranium mine, Denison Mines, Ltd. As chairman and chief executive officer of Denison, Roman has expanded the company into a diversified industrial firm with interests in oil and gas, coal, cement materials, and other mining and industrial investments throughout the free world.

Mr. Roman serves as a director of a number of business and philanthropic organizations, including the Guaranty Trust Company of Canada, the Crown Life Insurance Company, the Pacific Tin Consolidated Corporation, and the Canadian Nuclear Association. He is president of the Slovak World Congress, and honorary chairman of the Canadian Folk Arts Council.

In 1963, Pope John XXIII bestowed the order of Knight Commander of St. Gregory the Great on Mr. Roman, in recognition of his many years of devoted activity on behalf of the Catholic Church. He then became the only Canadian lay auditor to the Vatican Ecumenical Council in Rome in 1964.

Mr. Roman is married to the former Betty Gardon; they have four sons, three daughters, and three grandchildren. The Romans make their home at Romandale Farms in Unionville, on the outskirts of Toronto.

EUGEN LOEBL was born in 1907 in Slovakia. He received his degree from the University for World Trade in Vienna. By the 1930s, he had become one of Czechoslovakia's leading Marxist theoreticians. During the Nazi Occupation, Loebl went to London as head of the Ministry of Economic Reconstruction of the Czecho-Slovak Government in Exile; he also served as economic adviser to the Foreign Minister, Jan Masaryk, at UNRRA. After the war he became chief of the Ministry of Foreign Trade and a member of the Council of Economic Advisers of the Politburo. As part of his plan to help rebuild his country, he began to initiate trade with the United States and Western Europe. For this, he was arrested in 1949, interrogated brutally by Soviet intelligence officers, and forced to confess to a variety of fictionalized "crimes." He was tried during the infamous anti-Semitic Slansky Trials of 1952 and sentenced to life imprisonment. It was during five years of solitary confinement that he re-thought the theories of both communism and capitalism and developed the alternative system called Humanomics.

After eleven years in prison, he was released on probation in 1960 and forced to work as a manual laborer in a store-house. He was rehabilitated in 1963, and published his critique of Marxism, *Mental Work, The Real Source of Wealth*, which he had worked on and memorized during his solitary confinement. Loebl was appointed director of the State Bank in 1963. When the Soviets invaded Czechoslovakia in 1968, he fled to the West. After lecturing in Germany, he came to the United States, where he served for one semester as professor of economics at the University of Southern Illinois; then became professor of political science and economics at Vassar College until his retirement in 1976.

His books include: *Mental Work, The Real Source of Wealth; Stalinism in Prague; The Intellectual Revolution; Marxism, Boon or Dead End; Economy at the Crossroads; Humanomics;* and *My Mind on Trial.*

Commenting on *Humanomics,* Peter Drucker has said: "At last, a humanist economics—post-Marxian, post-Keynesian, an economics in which the human spirit and human knowledge are in the center. This is a truly important book, one that should make a profound and lasting impact." And Michael Novak hailed it as a "conceptual breakthrough" that "makes the mind long for further exploration."

Mr. Loebl is now at work developing specific, detailed applications of the ideas in *The Responsible Society*. He lives and works in New York City, with his wife, the painter Greta Schreyer. He is a member of the Board of Advisers of the Slovak World Congress.